Astrology & Predictions

Astrology & Predictions

The Predictive Techniques of

Ancient Scriptures: Redefined

Author

Ajay Srivastava

Jyotirvid, Jyotirvisharad

First Edition, 2024

Published by:

Ajay Kumar Srivastava

45, Awas Vikas Colony, Betiya Hata,

Gorakhpur – 273001 (U.P.), India

Mobile No.: +91-9867837184

Disclaimer: This publication contains the opinions and ideas of its author and is designed to provide useful information in regard to the subject matter covered. The author and the publisher specifically disclaim any responsibility for liability, loss, or risk, personal or otherwise, that is incurred as a consequence, directly or indirectly, of the use and application of any of the contents of this book.

<u>Lord Ganesha</u>

Prayer

ॐ नमो सिद्धि विनायकाय सर्व कार्य कर्त्रे सर्व विघ्न प्रशमनाय

सर्व राज्य वश्यकरणाय सर्वजन सर्वस्त्री पुरुष आकर्षणाय

श्रीं ॐ स्वाहा ।।

❙ Om Namo Siddhi Vinayakaya Sarva kaarya kartrey Sarva vighna prashamnay Sarvarjaya Vashyakarnaya Sarvajan Sarvastree Purush Aakarshanaya Shreeng Om Swaha ❙

(**Translation**: O Lord of Wisdom and Happiness, only you make every endeavor and everything possible. You are the remover of all obstacles and you have enchanted every being in the Universe, you are the Lord of all women and all men, Om Swaha.)

Dedication

I dedicate this book to my father (Late) Sri Ram Ashrey Lal Srivastava who taught me to be an independent, courageous and determined person, and my mother Maya Srivastava whose unconditional love and support always help me to overcome all the obstacles in my life. She has a selfless spirit and served others throughout her life. Her immense patience is peerless and she always inspires me to go ahead.

Preface

Astrology is deeply related with prediction; people are always eager to know what the future holds and what fate has in store for them. Therefore, many people think of astrology simply as a science of fortune-telling, and they are happy when they hear that their future will be bright. Its significance in their lives doesn't extend beyond this, and this esoteric science is nothing more than that to them. But the question arises that for what reason the person deserves that fortune, why some people have good fortune and others do not? Is that moving planets and stars play a vital role in deciding the fortune then why are there so much disparities in the world?

Many such questions arise and many people completely reject astrology and its principles and a few years ago I was also one of them. Later I started learning astrology and I remember that first time when I have written my first article about Ardra nakshatra in 2019, I couldn't muster the courage to tell anyone and it is kept in my computer for the next few months.

Slowly gathering courage, I told others, but no one took any interest, but later my predictions came true and that has given me courage to speak and write about astrology. As an avid student of astrology, gradually my collection of books became large and I found that for predictions it is necessary to first learn and experience the basics and not try to predict literally by reading scriptures.

People consider astrology as a part of entertainment and ask useless questions like where will they go today, what will they eat, what will they wear etc. This great science is not for such worthless questions and asking such questions shows the level of intelligence of the asking person.

When I started learning astrology I started compiling data from different sources. I come from the fields of Equity Research and Investment Banking, and I have conducted qualitative and quantitative analysis of numerous companies. While reading ancient texts, I found that they contained great information, and using my research skills, I analyzed this information in a spreadsheet and wrote down its meaning in simple language so that it can be understood even by those who are not aware of astrological concepts.

I added some techniques which I found during my analysis and these techniques will help in uncovering the secrets of a person's behavior. I hope that this book will be able to add a few drops to the unfathomable ocean of astrology.

Astrology is more complex than any other science. The palace of astrology which has collapsed needs to be rebuilt and according to the author it is the duty of every generation to work hard in this field. I hope that one day this great science will shine with its full grandeur.

I bow down to God for completing this book. Without the grace of the Almighty, it is not possible for me to express my thoughts in words.

Ajay Srivastava

March 7, 2024

Acknowledgement

The existence of this book would not have been possible without the help of my wife Seema and my daughter Saanvi. They provided me enough help to write down my thoughts which I have collected so far in my life. My wife has been instrumental as an illustrator and proof-reader and has given me enough insights to write the matter in a simple and explanatory manner.

Ajay Srivastava

Contents

Chapter 1

Introduction

Predictions in astrology are a continuous learning process and require not only analytical power but also the power of intuition. The constantly moving planets form different combinations and the energy level is changing every time and there is only one possibility for the event to occur among many combinations. An astrologer mind works to understand the working together of all these energies, yet the occurrence of an event is in the hands of God, therefore, many times intelligence fails and only intuition works.

Predictions are not merely about repeating the words written in our ancient texts, but about understanding the meaning of those words. The knowledge of astrology can help in unravelling the mysteries of the future. Every human being desire to know about the future, and this desire fuels the ongoing quest, a quest that ultimately leads them to explore the sky.

Man is always fascinated to see the stars in the sky. When the questions start arising about the effect of planets and stars and the person is not satisfied with the prevalent answers his gaze starts rising towards the sky and the search begin. The mysterious world of planets and stars starts attracting him, he sets out to find the answers and to discover the real truth.

Astrology is not a means of entertainment that we get on television and in newspapers. This great science is capable of providing answers to the unanswered questions of life, and until the person is not interested in finding these answers, they take astrology only for entertainment purposes.

Then the critics of astrology enter because whatever is available for entertainment can't last longer, because entertainment has no solid basis, and it cannot last for generations. Today, no one knows who those people were who were famous for entertaining others two or three generations ago, and who had millions of adoring fans. The current generation has completely forgotten them.

Vedic astrology is present for ages and people are always curious to know about their future. Curiosity turns into introspection for the seeker and they start studying the ancient science of India known as "Jyotish". The deeper one goes the more one realizes that the human mind cannot understand these mysteries, it is an unfathomable ocean and every dip in it reveals a new mystery.

Every step towards astrology has the potential to change a person. Just as each drop of a chemical changes the essence of the mixture, the person who moves on these steps is no longer the same person who started the journey. It is a long journey with no destination because when one reaches one destination the next goal is immediately ahead. Hence, astrology and spirituality are connected with each other and without being spiritual a person can't move forward on this path.

This journey starts opening secrets about the stars and planets and the seeker start realizing that we all are not living in isolation. These planets and stars are keeping a close eye on our every activity and our every action is being monitored and recorded. Whatever we do, we are responsible for suffering the consequences of that action then we should not do anything which we don't want to bear.

Hindu philosophy believes in the cycle of rebirth, so whatever left in this life a person carries all in the next life. It states that if you don't want to carry a negative karmic balance in your next life then you should not open an account with others where your liability is high. Without closing heavy liabilities, it is difficult for a person to watch on the sky and enter in the mysterious world of planets and stars. Liabilities must be settled first-and there is no escaping this. In the financial world, liabilities are legal obligations arising from past transactions that must be fulfilled to avoid bankruptcy or legal action. In precisely the same way, Nature, too, settles the accounts of the liabilities stemming from our actions-obligations from which no one can escape.

Every thought and action done by us has power to create an impact upon us and it is the soul which carries all for the next life. Human mind is extremally complex and it is difficult to get the answer that why a person behaves in a certain manner and why his behavior changes.

Astrology deals with the affairs of man and studies the influence of planets and stars on him. Human behavior is always complicated and it takes time to understand the behavior of the person, even there is no certainty. But astrology can give answer of these questions easily because behavior depends upon the planets and nakshatra placed in the horoscope. I discussed a technique in the next chapter that how to check the inclination and general disposition of the person after analyzing his horoscope.

The character of each individual plays a vital role in the choices he makes and astrology answers all these questions and also tells what a person's strengths and weaknesses are. The next important question is – whether events are fixed in our life or not, and if it is fixed then what is the meaning of doing our efforts and if it is not fixed then what is the meaning of astrological predictions.

I learned that something is certain and something is not. It is true that planets control our behavior but the choice to go up and down is always in our hands. This is the opportunity given by the nature to every human being which is not available to any other species. Whatever the decision we take and the direction we select, it paves the path for our next step and then it became fixed.

For example, a person got a wallet on the road with full of money, now he has a choice either to return it or keep it for himself. If he chooses to keep it then his Rahu will be strong and if he chooses to return the money then his Jupiter will become powerful and he cannot escape its result in the future. Rahu represents dishonesty and Jupiter represents honesty and it is in the hands of the person to choose the option of strengthening Rahu or Jupiter. Every act done by a person provides strength to planets and later it becomes his character.

We are familiar with numerous stories of both honesty and dishonesty in our lives. If an individual has worked with great integrity, it signifies that they have accumulated the assets of honesty in their life; conversely, if someone has engaged in theft or robbery, it implies that they have amassed the assets of dishonesty. Ultimately, every individual carries the assets and liabilities of their own actions.

Take another example of Mars the planet of energy and courage. If a person has shown an act of bravery it means he has collected coins of courage and remember that this is a continuation of the journey of previous lives. When the time comes to show courage in life and the person starts retreating then his Mars will become weak and when confronted Mars will be strong. This principle applies to every planet and our every action decides our next step. Hence, nature has given the choice in the hand of humans to select the direction of up or down and there is no limit of it.

Astrology considers five elements – fire, earth, air, water and ether for which the human body made and due to the combination of these elements a soul appears, a body exist and a mind function. Ether means space that presents everywhere and without space there is no action and no activity. Every horoscope represents the rest of the four elements and I discussed how to count the total weightage of each element because the disposition of the person shifts towards that which element weightage is high. I discussed few more techniques to find out the general disposition of the person.

Astrology not only deals with finding out the tendencies of the person but it provides the direction of choosing the right path in life. I am a person who wandered on many paths in my life. When I started writing books I realized that if I had not gone down those paths it would not have been possible for me to write at this stage of my life. I accepted that it was my fate to walk those paths and gain experience, later when I started learning astrology then all that experience is helping me to write my books.

A person selects to go on a path when he feels it is right but later when he realized that he is on the wrong path then he takes a U-turn. *I learn that nothing ends here; when one door is closed another door is waiting for your knocks and the door to learn the divine science never ends.* It is an endless journey, where everything is moving in a rotation and in that rotation, everything follow a certain principle. Human life is in search of freedom but every freedom demands sacrifices. This path is only for those who are ready for sacrifices.

When a person decides to learn astrology, they have to sacrifice a lot. During that time, he can do anything else. Like he can interact with his friends, he can go to watch a movie, he can do many other things but whatever option you choose will pave the way for the next selection.

There are many techniques of astrological predictions and I have been acquainted with them in many ways. Remember that predictions are not for fun. Astrology is not for the entertainment of people and the knowledge of this divine science should never be misused.

Lord Krishna says, "Whatever happened, happened for the good. Whatever is happening, is happening for the good. Whatever will happen, will also happen for the good. Do not weep for the past, do not worry for the future, concentrate on your present life." – Bhagavad Gita

Chapter 2

Techniques to Find
the
General Disposition

2.1 Elements of Sign & Planets

It is important to consider the elements of planets with the sign elements.

Elements of Signs

- **Fire:** Aries, Leo, Sagittarius

- **Earth:** Taurus, Virgo, Capricorn

- **Air:** Gemini, Libra, Aquarius

- **Water:** Cancer, Scorpio, Pisces

Elements of Planets

- Sun - Fire

- Moon – Water

- Mars – Fire

- Mercury - Earth

- Jupiter - Ether & Water

- Venus - Water

- Saturn – Air

A fiery planet in the fire sign becomes strong while the same planet in the water sign loses its strength. For example, Sun and Mars becomes strong in Aries but weak in Cancer.

2.2 Weightage of Each Element

Each planet in the horoscope placed in a house or bhavas (in Sanskrit) means – coming into existence. In astrology, the sky is divided into 12 zodiac signs and each sign is related to certain element like – fire, earth, air and water. The planets placed in these signs decide the total weightage of each element of the horoscope and thus decide the basic nature of the person. Each element produces certain disposition and a brief discussion about it is as follows;

2.2.1 Fire

Fire symbolizes beginnings, activity, and passion, so they are dynamic and courageous people. Fire indicates action and movement. They are leaders and pioneers and able to provide direction to others. Fire indicates transformation, purification and thrust for knowledge. This is a masculine and active energy and requires caution when handling fire. They never retrace their steps because the direction of fire is always upward. On the other hand, they are impatient and jump into action without proper thinking.

2.2.2 Earth

Earth sign indicates practical and grounded person. It is a feminine and passive energy that is incapable of taking initiative like fire sign. Therefore, safety comes first and these people prefer a middle path in their life. Earth indicates receptivity and patience; hence, these people analyze every fact and figure before taking any decision. They seek prosperity and work hard to improve and secure their financial position.

2.2.3 Air

These people are intelligent with strong analytical abilities. When air circulates, it is fresh, when it gets stuck in a place, it starts giving foul smell. Therefore, these people lack stability, are unable to sit at one place and prefer to wander here and there. They are witty individuals and are strong in communication.

2.2.4 Water

This sign indicates a very sensitive, emotional and moody person. They are not rigid as water changes its shape quickly. Their intuition is very strong as water picks up vibrations quickly. Water has nurturing qualities so they are helpful people and considerate of others.

For a balanced personality, equal importance of all four elements is necessary. Due to increase or decrease of any element, a person's behavior is affected accordingly.

2.3 Qualities of Signs

Not only the element but each sign also assigned a quality. There are three types of qualities – Movable, Fixed and Dual (Common or Mutable).

2.3.1 Movable

Aries, Cancer, Libra, Capricorn

As the name suggests, these people easily adapt to new situations and find their own way out of a problem rather than waiting for a person or a particular time. They like change, take initiative and encourage others. They are goal-oriented individuals and flow with purpose in life. They accept challenges and look for new opportunities instead of holding back.

The movable sign indicates a new beginning and their every beginning begins with change. Like a new season begins but it is the end of the previous season. This indicates that they are leaders and trendsetters who remove old things and implement new changes. But every change carries some risk and if the person is not able to assess it, the result creates problems for many people. Therefore, they are visionary individuals who properly understand the risks involved in the task. As the seasons change with the movement of the Sun, they implement new ideas and bring about change.

On the other hand, it indicates an impulsive and dissatisfied person who takes worthless initiatives, is restless and gets easily agitated. They waste their energy in worthless wandering and ultimately get no results.

2.3.2 Fixed

Taurus, Leo, Scorpio, Aquarius

They are stable and consistent people. They are loyal and remain firm on their decisions. They believe in their tradition and do not like change. Their nature is to do everything fix, so that there is no further risk. They are perfectionists, work hard and complete tasks with utmost dedication. They do not like anything half-baked, be it work or relationship, and when the reaction of the other person is lackluster, they leave it forever.

They know how to maintain things and keep things safe but they are unable to take initiation. They like to follow the action plan without any change, prioritize safety first and prefer to stay in the middle as there are chances of falling off to the side. Therefore, they choose only those options where the risk is minimal and no chance of any loss.

On the other hand, they are stubborn individuals who do not like to change their opinions. They also cling to negative things and find it very difficult to let them go.

2.3.3 Dual

Gemini, Virgo, Sagittarius, Pisces

It is also known as common or mutable sign. The word dual means related to two. When two parts or aspects of something come together it indicates duality in their personality. This means that they can do two things at the same time. Like a chameleon changes its color according to the situation, although this is taken in a negative sense, but in other words it adapts itself to the situation without complaining. Therefore, these people adjust to the situation and have the ability to adapt quickly to changing circumstances without any complain. These qualities indicate that they are very flexible and versatile person.

The meaning of dual nature is neither mobile nor stable but it is a mixture of both and one of them comes to the fore when the situation demands. The changed behavior of the person may surprise others that what was previously rigid is now showing dynamic tendencies, but everything depends on the circumstances. Therefore, these people immediately sense the change in circumstances even before it occurs and prepare everything in advance for safety, just like a chameleon changes its color quickly and is able to hide from the eyes of others.

On the other hand, they are able to hide their true face and can easily deceive others. It also shows the selfish nature of the person. The person who was very sociable at one time, his behavior suddenly changes and the second behavior is completely different from the previous one. Due to circumstances, his second aspect has now come to the surface and that is completely different from the first aspect.

Movable zodiac signs are initial signs, fixed zodiac signs come under the middle and dual zodiac signs indicate the end. The Sun enters Aries on 14 April and Pisces on 15 March and completes a cycle of rotation from movable sign to dual sign. When the Sun enters the movable (chara) sign, four seasons start respectively - spring, summer, autumn and winter.

These three qualities (movable, fixed and dual) define the overall personality of a person and overall weightage of all the three indicates the strengths and weaknesses of the person. It should be remembered that excess of one quality means deficiency of other.

Therefore, proper balance of all three qualities and four elements is necessary as shift towards one quality or element indicates work-life imbalance and without knowing the root cause it is difficult to achieve a balanced personality. Now we will discuss about how to calculate it with the help of a horoscope.

Table 1:

No.	Sign	Element	Quality
1	Aries	Fire	Movable
2	Taurus	Earth	Fixed
3	Gemini	Air	Dual
4	Cancer	Water	Movable
5	Leo	Fire	Fixed
6	Virgo	Earth	Dual
7	Libra	Air	Movable
8	Scorpio	Water	Fixed
9	Sagittarius	Fire	Dual
10	Capricorn	Earth	Movable
11	Aquarius	Air	Fixed
12	Pisces	Water	Dual

2.4 Count of Elements

The total count of the elements is 12 (excluding (Uranus, Neptune and Pluto), and calculated as follows;

Total 9 Planets = 9 Points

Ascendant = 1 Point

Meridian Cusp (Mc) = 1 Point;

Formula for Mc = (Asc. – 90°)

Fortuna = 1 Point;

Formula for Fortuna = (Ascendant + Moon – Sun)

12 Points = 9 Planets+Ascendant+Mc+Fortuna

Example Chart 1:

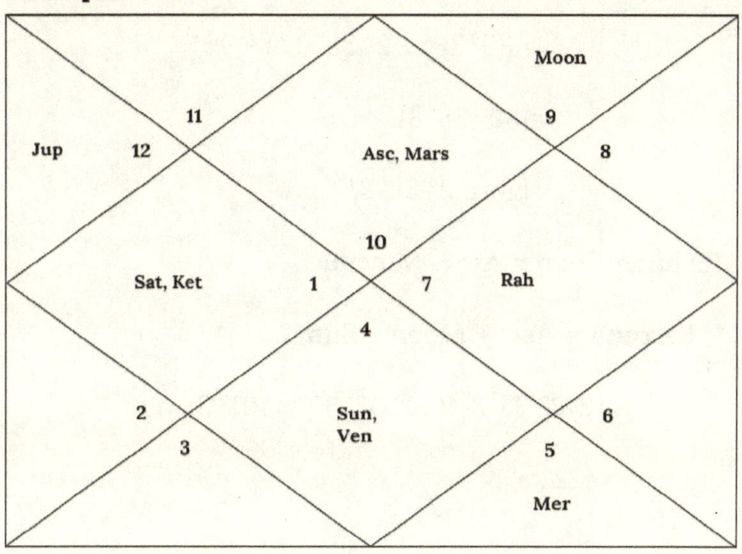

No.	Planets	Signs	Degree	Element	Quality
1	Asc.	Capricorn	2:28:31	Earth	Movable
2	Sun	Cancer	11:31:39	Water	Movable
3	Moon	Sagittarius	10:58:39	Fire	Dual
4	Mars (R)	Capricorn	5:10:01	Earth	Movable
5	Mercury (R)	Leo	1:10:49	Fire	Fixed
6	Jupiter	Pisces	15:46:38	Water	Dual
7	Venus	Cancer	00:46:24	Water	Movable
8	Saturn	Aries	8:01:47	Fire	Movable
9	Rahu (R)	Libra	10:50:58	Air	Movable
10	Ketu (R)	Aries	10:50:58	Fire	Movable

11. Meridian Cusp = (Asc. - 90°)

$$= ((9*30) + 2° 38' 31") - 90°$$

$$=182° 38' 31"$$

$$=Libra\ 2° 38' 31"$$

Meridian Cusp = Air & Movable

12. Fortuna = Asc. + Moon - Sun

$$=272° 38' 3+250° 58' 39" - 101° 31' 39"$$

$$=422° 5' 3"$$

$$=62° 5' 3"$$

$$=Gemini\ 2° 5' 3"$$

Fortuna = Air & Dual

(**Note:** Add 360° if the result is negative and reduce 360° if the result is more than 360°)

Now, calculate the above points as per the table given below;

Element	Fire	Earth	Air	Water	Sum	Percentage
Movable	2	2	2	2	8	67%
Fixed	1	0	0	0	1	8%
Dual	1	0	1	1	3	25%
Sum	4	2	3	3	12	
Percentage	33%	17%	25%	25%		100%

The following charts clearly show the contribution of each element in the personality of the person.

Element

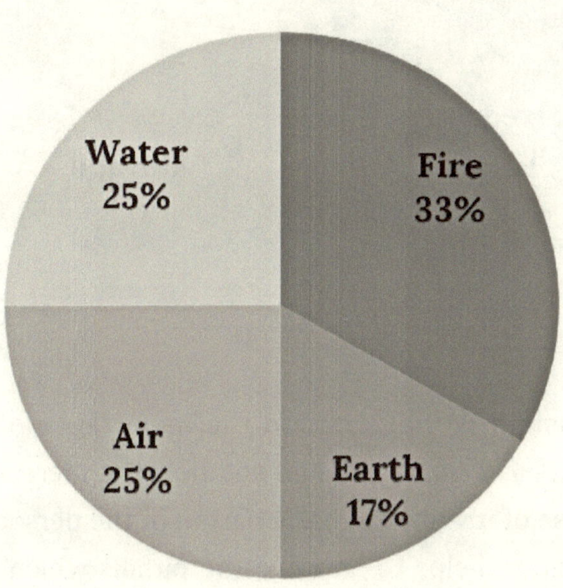

<u>Quality of Signs</u>

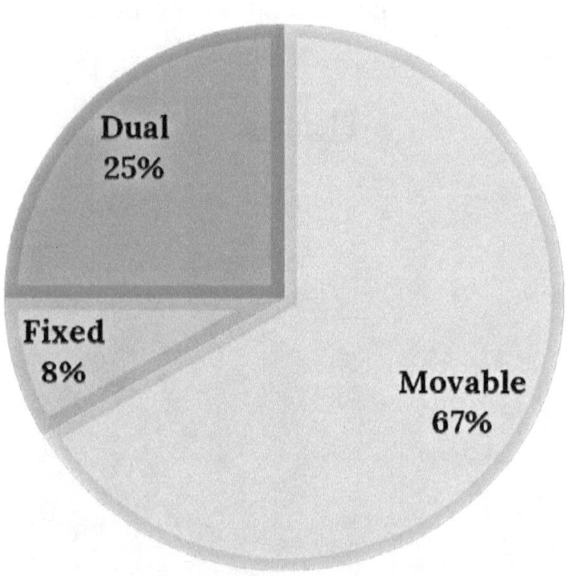

Conclusion: We understood the importance of each elements and quality of sign and how the increase and decrease of it, shift the basic nature of the person. This information helps to improve the pitfalls which might the person himself is not aware of that.

In the above chart the high percentage of fire and movable sign indicates a very active person but the percentage of fixed sign is only 8% indicates that such person is unable to retain things. Therefore, any step taken without proper consideration of all the pros and cons does not yield proper results.

Chapter 3

Total Count of Qualities of Nakshatra

In this chapter we will learn how the total count of the characteristics of Nakshatras plays an important role. Hence, it is important to understand the Nakshatras and the total count of their characteristic provide the inherent inclination of the person and thus determines the purpose of his life.

Each nakshatra and each planet in the horoscope represents a specific energy. The planets are in fact the transformers of that energy and every Nakshatra has a certain characteristic with an emphasis on a goal. The horoscope of a person is a combination of the energy of nine planets and behind that the energy of Nakshatras works.

There are many qualities of Nakshatra but here we will consider eight main qualities. Below is a brief outline of these qualities;

3.1 Caste – All 27 Nakshatras are divided into seven castes.

i) Brahmin Nakshatra – Krittika, Purva Phalguni, Purva Ashadha, Purva Bhadrapada

Brahmin (Scholar) Nakshatra indicates that they are inclined towards knowledge and wisdom. They are a spiritual, intellectual, and liberal person. Learning is a lifelong process and a Brahmin never stops learning and they learn quickly. Brahmin is a person;

1. Who works with his mind and can think deeply.

2. They can generate new and innovative ideas.

3. They have a philosophical outlook and are always thirsty for knowledge.

4. They are a knowledgeable and visionary person and can provide good advice from their wisdom.

5. Brahmin shows the right direction of life. Jupiter is a brahmin planet and the index finger represents Jupiter. Therefore, when a person shows direction to others he uses his index finger.

6. They prefer to achieve their goals by working on a strategy and never take impulsive actions.

7. If the present time is not favorable for them, then they prefer to keep quiet, but their mind is always engaged in making strategies and they implement them only when the time is favorable. This shows their quality of patience.

ii) Kshatriya (Warrior) Nakshatra – Pushya, Uttara Phalguni, Uttara Ashadha, Uttara Bhadrapada

Kshatriya (Warrior) Nakshatra indicates that they are good in administration, politics and governance. They are very active people and aggressive by nature. They are determined, courageous people who serve as protectors and are ready to fight for justice. A warrior is one who;

1. Warriors are those whose ultimate aim is to win the battle. They don't settle for less than victory.

2. Warriors are belligerent, they have a strong ability to survive in difficult times. Once decided a warrior never deviate from the chosen path.

3. They are ready to bear any pain to achieve the objective, mission is always important to them.

4. They are dedicated to their goal. They never retrace their steps and find their own way to continue their journey towards achievement of the goal.

5. They are focused and disciplined person.

6. They are not interested in dealings and negotiations.

7. They are duty bound person and never wave to fulfill their duty.

iii). Vaishya Nakshatra – Ashwini, Punarvasu, Hasta

Vaishya (Merchant) Nakshatra indicates that the person has natural interest in trade and business. They understand financial matters quickly, are good at negotiations and avoid conflicts.

Merchants are the provider of necessary means to society but in exchange for that, they want something in their pocket. A merchant is that person;

1. Who is not aggressive and uses gentle words.

2. One who is proficient in dealings.

3. One who knows better the time value of money.

4. One who can recognize the hidden value of a thing and has patience for its fruits.

5. One who knows about the surroundings, environment, and place of the goods produced.

6. One who is willing to cooperate with others.

7. One who is willing to go anywhere for a good deal.

8. One who can adapt quickly to changing times and is ready to let go of the past without attachment.

9. One who does not have the arrogance to meet anyone from business perspective.

10. One who is not easily discouraged by unsuccessful attempts.

11. One who respects talent and is willing to pay for it.

Balance is the most important thing in business and those who maintain balance and avoid conflict are the ones who succeed in business.

iv) Shudra Nakshatra – Rohini, Magha, Anuradha, Revati

Shudra (servant / support) is not the downtrodden person of the society as people generally think. They are very hardworking people and provide their services to others with the help of their legs. They are ready to follow the orders of their master. Shudra is one;

1. Whose legs are strong.

2. They make an infertile land into a fertile land with their hard work and feed the people.

3. They play a vital role in the society as well as the economy. They run around to supply all the essential things. They are the pillars of the society.

4. They take care of every person in the family, and supply all the required things.

5. To fulfill their obligation, they never take rest and work for long hours.

6. They are individuals who are determined to help, overcome every obstacle and emerge victorious with their hard work.

7. In corporate world, when one meeting is over they run for another meeting and the third and the fourth is also scheduled. Only a person with very strong legs can do this.

No wonder that the Magha Nakshatra whose symbol is "throne" has been given the "Shudra" caste by the ancient sages. A king has to move from one place to another and observe everything for its proper functioning.

When there is energy in the legs, such a person cannot sit quietly. This energy forces him to move and such a person is best suited for jobs where high movement is required.

v) Mleccha (Outcaste) Nakshatra – Bharani, Aslesha, Vishakha, Shravana

This wild energy works to perform tasks that traditional society does not generally accept. They like to do those works which other people are not ready to do. They feel no shame in working with primitive human instincts which have an element of excitement, adventure and provide a thrill. This energy creates an attraction that enables these people to remain isolated from others as well as conceal their actions.

In society, people want to release their suppressed energy and are looking for this excitement. Products that can create such a thrill are in great demand. When people are suddenly exposed to a shocking thing they feel instantly attracted and this energy (Mleccha) knows how to use these stimuli. Therefore, Mleccha people have the quality to make things exciting and they are the creators of exciting news. Due to their extraordinary quality, they can attract the attention of others. They know what to do to attract people, therefore, they are not bothered about controversies.

In the present days, these characteristics make these people come "On top of every caste" rather than outcaste. They are famous performers, artists, celebrities, and work for media and entertainment, and other industries where these types of work are required to attract the masses. They invite shocking facts and controversial things, which create uproar and excitement among the public. They remain on top of the news channels with their antics.

To increase sales, companies are looking for activities that create excitement among people and fascinate them to buy the product. Therefore, the people who can create such type of excitement are in great demand by these companies.

People of these Nakshatras discard the mainstream function of family or society and engage in activities that are not accepted by traditional society. They like excitement and adventure and love to perform such acts. Some other characteristics of the Mlecchas are as follows:

- They form personal relationships with people who do not belong to their society, community, or country.

- They like to marry foreigners or a person who is not from their religion or culture or society.

- They do not want to follow the law and culture of their tradition and often say that they do not believe in casteism and stereotypes and they want to live their lives freely. Therefore, they prefer to live their separate lives.

Mleccha energy seeks and creates that attraction that no other energy can provide. This energy is capable of doing something exciting and to which the person is attracted. This energy separates itself from the things that people in society generally follow. Controlled energy can yield positive results, so physical activities, sports, dance, and meditation are essential for these people. Otherwise, it is wasted in creating controversy and enjoying the thrill, but the thrill is fleeting. That's why they keep looking for one thrill after another and being in controversies becomes the purpose of their life.

Constantly chasing after fleeting things leaves a deep imprint on the mind, and at times, these individuals begin to lose control over their minds and start behaving like eccentrics. Despite the name and fame, that intense and unnatural life, often fraught with controversy, gives rise to a deep and enduring loneliness. Therefore, after getting much success in the outer world, these people often feel empty inside.

On the higher aspect, these nakshatras have a strong capacity for self-expression that does not accept social constraints. However, the path to its execution may be full of controversies, but it is the pursuit of freedom and the greatest freedom is the freedom of the soul from birth and death. Therefore, Mleccha energies have a strong potential to produce great sages.

Four Phases of Mleccha Energy;

a) Bharani – It is an inexperienced, young, and enthusiastic energy that requires guidance. They are eager and ready to learn and gather wisdom through experience.

b) Ashlesha – It is the energy that likes to break the rules, it has gained experience but still needs maturity.

c) Vishakha - This is an extremely wild and powerful energy. Here a powerful manifestation is seen who can do anything to achieve what it wants. It is a strong transformative energy that transcends any limits.

Therefore, the path of truth is essential for these people and when transformed it can lead to great spirituality.

d) Shravana - This is the most mature energy which has experience as well as efficiency. This energy goes deep and creates an understanding of deep spiritual meanings. This powerful energy has developed wisdom by gaining control of their own vibration.

This is the most developed stage of all Mleccha energies where the individual follows spiritual rituals and organizes his energies.

vi) Servant Nakshatra – Mrigshira, Chitra, Jyeshtha, Dhanishta

The important qualities of these Nakshatras are integrity and commitment. These people provide all possible help and adapt themselves according to the circumstances. These people are flexible and are ready to listen to others. A servant is one;

1. Who rushes to complete the work as soon as he hears the signal from the master and waits till he gets the signal. Therefore, these people have sharp senses to catch the signals and they understand the situation before others.

2. These people are very good at anticipating the situations and planning accordingly. They contribute with their high quality in making the work successful.

3. Servants keep running for the work of others. Hence, these people like to travel. They prefer short-duration meetings from one place to another but they cannot sit in one place for a long time. They are the best people for jobs where traveling is important.

4. Servants never wait for the last moment and prepare everything in advance to fulfill the wish of their master. Similarly, these people never do any work in a hurry and haphazardly, they perfectly prepare everything. They have a strong ability to use every available resource to get the work done.

5. They are always ready to listen to the complaints of others and make every possible effort to solve the problem. They are best suited for jobs that require public dealing where the person listens to the complaint calmly and resolves it. This is the same quality of a servant who listens to his master's complaint calmly and resolves it.

vii) Butcher Nakshatra – Ardra, Swati, Mula, Satabhisha

It is a fierce energy. A butcher is a person;

1. A butcher deals with flesh and blood and cuts the flesh mercilessly.

2. Their eyes are penetrating and their hands are powerful.

3. Those who show no mercy while causing destruction and act in a very harsh manner.

4. They become ruthless when removal is important to achieve the final result.

5. When it becomes necessary to cut something off these people do not hesitate to do so. They end relationships, break old friendships, end discussions abruptly, and walk out of meetings.

6. They have no sympathy for the past; if the present situation demands separation from anything, then they do it immediately.

7. To get their work done, they never hesitate to cut whatever obstructs them. They may immediately cut their long ties with the one obstructing their way, but achieving the goal is always important to them.

8. Medical surgeons belong to the butcher caste, and surgery is an act in which no mercy is shown to the patient. They use their skills to save lives by removing harmful things from the body.

3.2 Nature – There are seven nature of Nakshatras.

i) Kshipra (Swift) Nakshatra – Ashwini, Pushya, Hasta

These nakshatra indicates activities related with swiftness where growth and development are involved. They want quick results and are intense to achieve their objective.

ii) Mridu (Soft) Nakshatra – Mrigashira, Chitra, Anuradha, Revati

This nakshatra indicates strong sensitivity and power to catch subtle things. As such, an artist has tender qualities and is able to capture subtle moves and vibrations.

iii) Mixed (Sharp & Soft) Nakshatra – Krittika, Vishakha

These nakshatra combine both qualities of sharpness and softness but only one on the surface. These people carry out normal activities peacefully but when the situation demands, they take drastic measures to overcome the problem. Like someone was laughing at the table but in the next movement he took a sharp knife in his hand.

iv) Dhruva (Fixed) Nakshatra – Rohini, Uttara Phalguni, Uttara Ashadha, Shravana, Uttara Bhadrapada

It indicates activities where things need to be fixed permanently, such as a house being fixed to one place. These people are good for work that requires laying a strong foundation.

v) Ugra (Dreadful) Nakshatra – Bharani, Magha, Purva Phalguni, Purva Ashadha, Purva Bhadrapada

These nakshatras are good for fierce activities and indicate use of force.

vi) Tikshna (Sharp) Nakshatra – Ardra, Aslesha, Jyeshtha, Mula

These nakshatras are good for activities related with separation and indicate a person who doesn't think twice to separate something.

vii) Chara (Movable) Nakshatra – Punarvasu, Swati, Dhanishta, Satabhisha

It indicates movement and these people are unable to stay at one place for long time, like a vehicle requires movement.

3.3 Activity – There are three types of activity.

i) Active Nakshatra – Krittika, Aslesha, Magha, Chitra, Vishakha, Jyeshtha, Mula, Dhanishta, Satabhisha

They are energetic person and like to take initiative.

ii) Passive Nakshatra – Ashwini, Mrigashira, Punarvasu, Pushya, Hasta, Swati, Anuradha, Shravana It indicates the receptivity of the person. These people require motivation to produce results otherwise they remain in a state of silence.

iii) Balanced Nakshatra – Bharani, Rohini, Ardra, Purva Phalguni, Uttara Phalguni, Purva Ashadha, Uttara Ashadha, Purva Bhadrapada, Uttara Bhadrapada, Revati

These nakshatras have both the above qualities and show the outcome depending upon need. They think all pros and cons before taking any action and do not react suddenly. They always try to bring balance when the scale of the situation shifts in one direction.

3.4 TriMurti - There are three types of TriMurti.

i) Brahma (Creation) Nakshatra – Ashwini, Rohini, Punarvasu, Magha, Hasta,

Vishakha, Mula, Shravana, Purva Bhadrapada

Brahma Nakshatra indicates the ability to create and these people always think in a constructive manner.

ii) Vishnu (Maintenance) Nakshatra – Bharani, Mrigashira, Pushya, Purva Phalguni, Chitra, Anuradha, Purva Ashadha, Dhanishta, Uttara Bhadrapada

Vishnu Nakshatra indicates the ability to maintain. They are always thinking about growth and sustainability. If there is life then there is movement, hence these people give speed to the stalled things. They are very active person and hate anything idle.

iii) Mahesh (Destruction) Nakshatra – Krittika, Ardra, Aslesha, Uttara Phalguni, Swati, Jyeshtha, Uttara Ashadha, Shatabhisha, Revati

These nakshatra indicates quality of dissolution. Along with construction, destruction is also a part of nature and these nakshatra participate in those activities. It indicates a person who does not hesitate to cut something or put the things to its end.

3.5 Gender - There are three types of gender.

i) Male Nakshatra – Ashwini, Pushya, Punarvasu, Hasta, Anuradha, Shravana, Purva Bhadrapada, Uttara Bhadrapada

It indicates masculine activities. More count of masculine nakshatra indicates aggressive tendencies of the person.

ii) Female Nakshatra – Bharani, Krittika, Rohini, Ardra, Aslesha, Magha, Purva Phalguni, Uttara Phalguni, Chitra, Swati, Vishakha, Jyeshtha, Purva Ashadha, Uttara Ashadha, Dhanishta, Revati

It indicates feminine activities. More count of feminine nakshatra indicates receptive tendencies of the person.

iii) Neuter Nakshatra – Mrigashira, Mula, Satabhisha

It indicates harsh activities. If the count of neuter nakshatra is high then the person is cruel. It also indicates that the planets which are in these Nakshatras and the houses in which they are placed, the person have no attachment to those matters and he becomes ruthless.

3.6 Gana (Type) – There are three types of ganas.

i) Dev (Deity) Nakshatra – Ashwini, Mrigashira, Punarvasu, Pushya, Hasta, Swati, Anuradha, Shravana, Revati

The dev nakshatra indicates work for the betterment of others without expectations. They are soft-spoken and generous people with virtuous qualities.

ii) Manushya (Human) Nakshatra – Bharani, Rohini, Ardra, Purva Phalguni, Uttara Phalguni, Purva Ashadha, Uttara Ashadha, Purva Bhadrapada, Uttara Bhadrapada

Humans are the middle between gods and devils, hence they have mix qualities. They have humanitarian qualities and try to bring balance in life and sometimes they become extremally rigid.

iii) Rakshasa (Demon) Nakshatra – Krittika, Aslesha, Magha, Chitra, Vishakha, Jyeshtha, Mula, Dhanishta, Satabhisha

These people are interested in nature and work as its protectors. They are very energetic but need motivation for work and do not take initiative without personal gain.

3.7 Guna (Quality) - There are three types of gunas.

i) Rajasic – Rajas means action. These nakshatra indicates very active person and take initiative to get the desires fulfilled.

ii) Tamasic – Tamas means inaction. These nakshatra indicates darkness, inaction, and laziness.

iii) Satwic – Sattva means knowledge and intelligence. This nakshatra indicates a generous person with spiritual inclination and the quality of forgiveness.

3.8 Nakshatra Goal - There are four types of nakshatra goal.

i) Dharma (Righteousness) – The right way to live life. To follow the laws of nature and make every possible effort to protect it.

ii) Artha (Economic values)– To live with respect in this world, money is needed and for that, skill is needed. Artha means to achieve it without being greedy.

iii) Kama (Desire) – People keep searching for pleasure without which the person becomes dry and empty. Kama is related to sensuality but it has broad meaning and it is related to art, music, love and affection.

iv) Moskha (Liberation) – It means freedom but without sacrifice there is no freedom. These nakshatra indicates that the person will sacrifice material things in search of higher things in life.

3.9 Pada Goal - Pada has also the four goals; Pada 1 - Dharma, Pada 2 - Artha, Pada 3 - Kama, Pada 4 - Moskha. The total weightage of these pada provides the subtle view of nakshatra goal.

For example; suppose in a chart the nakshatra goal is Dharma – 20%, Artha -20%, Kama – 40%, and Moskha – 20% and the pada goal is Dharma – 20%, Artha -20%, Kama – 20%, and Moskha – 40%.

In pada goal, the percentage of Moksha has increased and the percentage of Kama decreased. It means that the person will do sacrifice for his pleasure when such type of situation arises in his life and vice versa. The information of pada provides subtle information about the behavior of the person.

(**Note:** *To know more about Nakshatra readers can refer my book "The Light of Nakshatras".*)

Table 2: Nakshatra and its Various Properties

Nakshatra	Caste	Nature	Activity	TriMurti	Gender	Gana	Guna	Naksh. Goal
Ashwini	Vaishya	Swift	Passive	Brahma	Male	Deva	Rajasic	Dharma
Bharani	Mleccha	Ugra	Balanced	Vishnu	Female	Manushya	Tamasic	Artha
Krittika	Brahmin	Mixed	Active	Shiva	Female	Rakshasa	Satwic	Kama
Rohini	Shudra	Dhruva	Balanced	Brahma	Female	Manushya	Rajasic	Moksha
Mrigashira	Servant	Mridu	Passive	Vishnu	Neuter	Deva	Tamasic	Moksha
Ardra	Butcher	Tikshna	Balanced	Shiva	Female	Manushya	Satwic	Kama
Punarvasu	Vaishya	Chara	Passive	Brahma	Male	Deva	Rajasic	Artha
Pushya	Kshatriya	Swift	Passive	Vishnu	Male	Deva	Tamasic	Dharma
Aslesha	Mleccha	Tikshna	Active	Shiva	Female	Rakshasa	Satwic	Dharma
Magha	Shudra	Ugra	Active	Brahma	Female	Rakshasa	Rajasic	Artha
P. Phalguni	Brahmin	Ugra	Balanced	Vishnu	Female	Manushya	Tamasic	Kama
U. Phalguni	Kshatriya	Dhruva	Balanced	Shiva	Female	Manushya	Satwic	Moksha
Hasta	Vaishya	Swift	Passive	Brahma	Male	Deva	Rajasic	Moksha
Chitra	Servant	Mridu	Active	Vishnu	Female	Rakshasa	Tamasic	Kama
Swati	Butcher	Chara	Passive	Shiva	Female	Deva	Satwic	Artha
Vishakha	Mleccha	Mixed	Active	Brahma	Female	Rakshasa	Rajasic	Dharma
Anuradha	Shudra	Mridu	Passive	Vishnu	Male	Deva	Tamasic	Dharma
Jyeshtha	Servant	Tikshna	Active	Shiva	Female	Rakshasa	Satwic	Artha
Mula	Butcher	Tikshna	Active	Brahma	Neuter	Rakshasa	Rajasic	Kama
P. Ashadha	Brahmin	Ugra	Balanced	Vishnu	Female	Manushya	Tamasic	Moksha
U. Ashadha	Kshatriya	Dhruva	Balanced	Shiva	Female	Manushya	Satwic	Moksha
Shravana	Mleccha	Dhruva	Passive	Brahma	Male	Deva	Rajasic	Artha
Dhanishta	Servant	Chara	Active	Vishnu	Female	Rakshasa	Tamasic	Dharma
Satabhisha	Butcher	Chara	Active	Shiva	Neuter	Rakshasa	Satwic	Dharma
P. Bhadrapada	Brahmin	Ugra	Passive	Brahma	Male	Manushya	Rajasic	Artha
U. Bhadrapada	Kshatriya	Dhruva	Balanced	Vishnu	Male	Manushya	Tamasic	Kama
Revati	Shudra	Mridu	Balanced	Shiva	Female	Deva	Satwic	Moksha

Example Chart: Refer to the example chart 1 (page 31) in chapter 2, below is the position of planets, nakshatra and pada.

No.	Planets	Nakshatra	Pada	Pada Goal
1	Asc.	Uttara Ashadha	2	Artha
2	Sun	Pushya	3	Kama
3	Moon	Mula	4	Moksha
4	Mars (R)	Uttara Ashadha	3	Kama
5	Mercury (R)	Magha	1	Dharma
6	Jupiter	Uttara Bhadrapada	4	Moksha
7	Venus	Pururvasu	4	Moksha
8	Saturn	Ashwini	3	Kama
9	Rahu (R)	Swati	2	Artha
10	Ketu (R)	Ashwini	4	Moksha

With the help of Table 2, we can easily identify the qualities of the Nakshatra present in example chart 1.

Nakshatra	Caste	Nature	Activity	TriMurti	Gender	Gana	Guna	Nak. Goal	Pada Goal
U. Ashadha	Kshatriya	Dhruva	Balanced	Shiva	Female	Manushya	Satwic	Moksha	Artha
Pushya	Kshatriya	Swift	Passive	Vishnu	Male	Deva	Tamasic	Dharma	Kama
Mula	Butcher	Tikshna	Active	Brahma	Neuter	Rakshasa	Rajasic	Kama	Moksha
U. Ashadha	Kshatriya	Dhruva	Balanced	Shiva	Female	Manushya	Satwic	Moksha	Kama
Magha	Shudra	Ugra	Active	Brahma	Female	Rakshasa	Rajasic	Artha	Dharma
U. Bhadrapada	Kshatriya	Dhruva	Balanced	Vishnu	Male	Manushya	Tamasic	Kama	Moksha
Pururvasu	Vaishya	Chara	Passive	Brahma	Male	Deva	Rajasic	Artha	Moksha
Ashwini	Vaishya	Swift	Passive	Brahma	Male	Deva	Rajasic	Dharma	Kama
Swati	Butcher	Chara	Passive	Shiva	Female	Deva	Satwic	Artha	Artha
Ashwini	Vaishya	Swift	Passive	Brahma	Male	Deva	Rajasic	Dharma	Moksha

Now we will count all the qualities and convert them into percentage. Every person has a mixture of different qualities and the qualities that count more are present on the surface of the personality. Each of the qualities written in the above table are present in a person and they come in front at the right time in life.

1. Caste	Brahmin	Kshatriya	Vaishya	Shudra	Mleccha	Servant	Butcher	Total
Count	0	4	3	1	0	0	2	10
Percentage	0%	40%	30%	10%	0%	0%	20%	100%

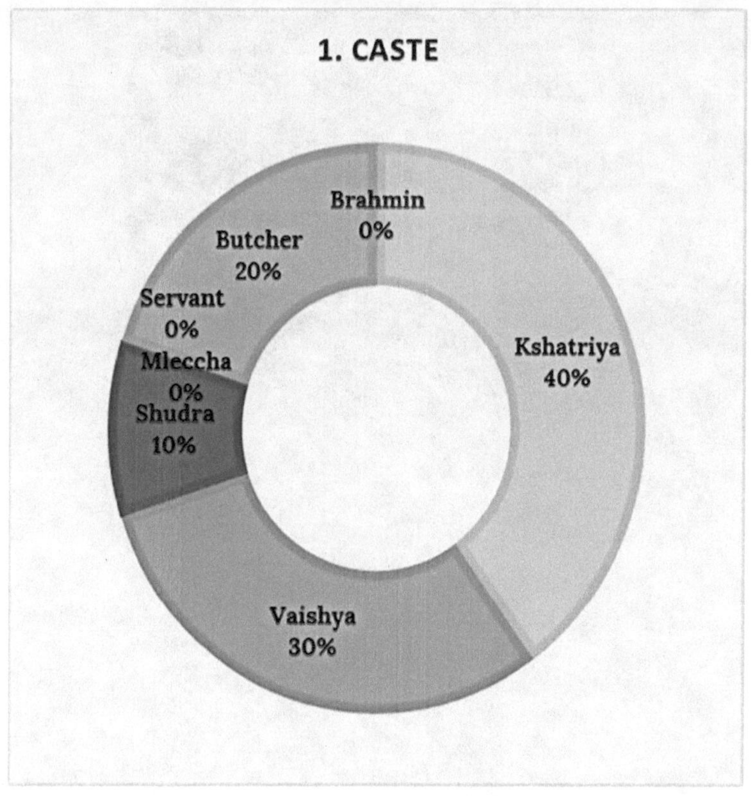

2. Nature	Swift	Ugra	Mixed	Dhruva	Mridu	Tikshna	Chara	Total
Count	3	1	0	3	0	1	2	10
Percentage	30%	10%	0%	30%	0%	10%	20%	100%

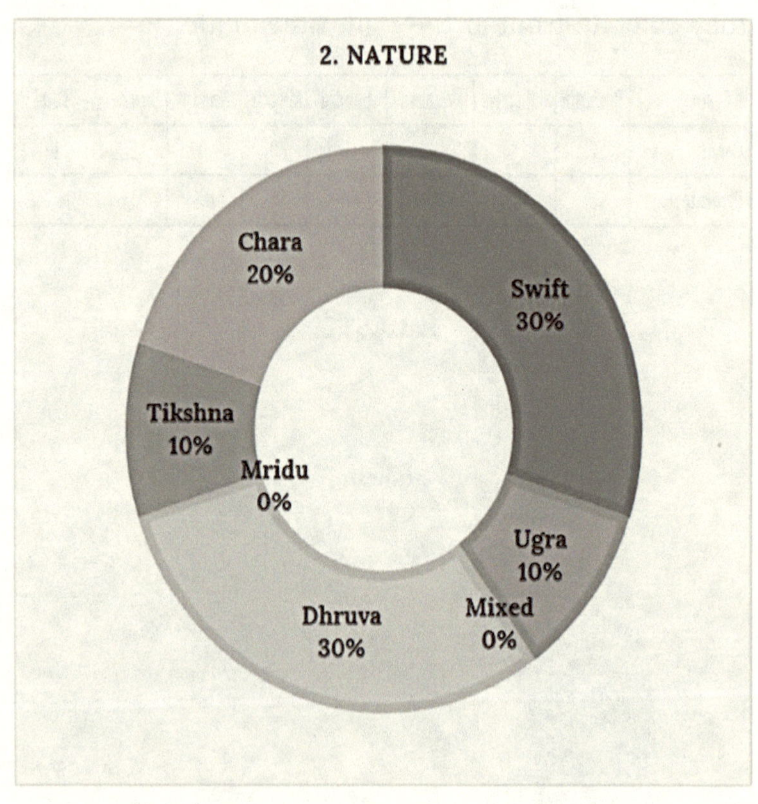

3. Activity	Active	Passive	Balanced	Total
Count	2	5	3	10
Percentage	20%	**50%**	30%	100%

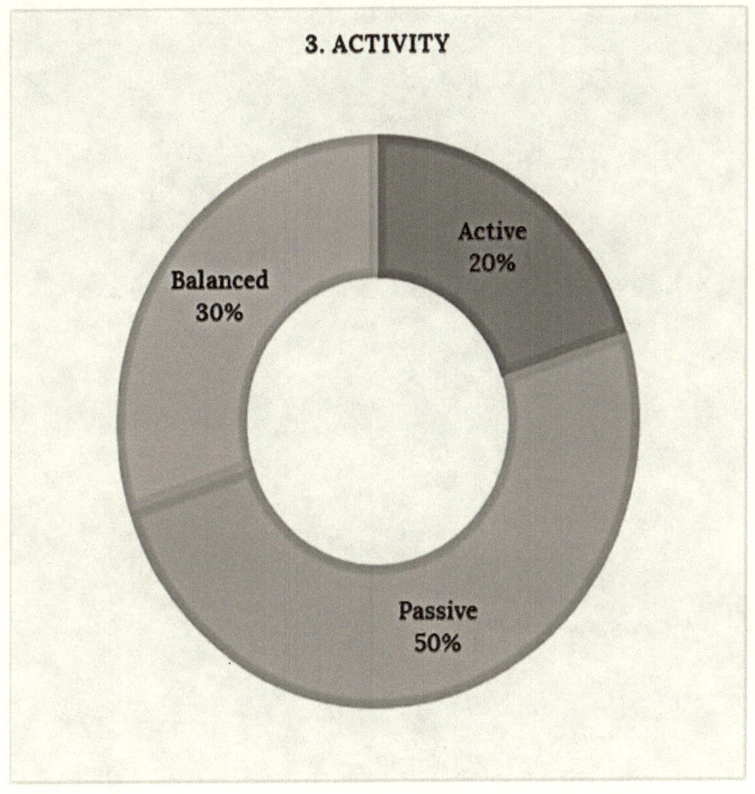

4. TriMurti	Brahma - Creation	Vishnu - Maintenance	Shiva - Dissolution	Total
Count	5	2	3	10
Percentage	50%	20%	30%	100%

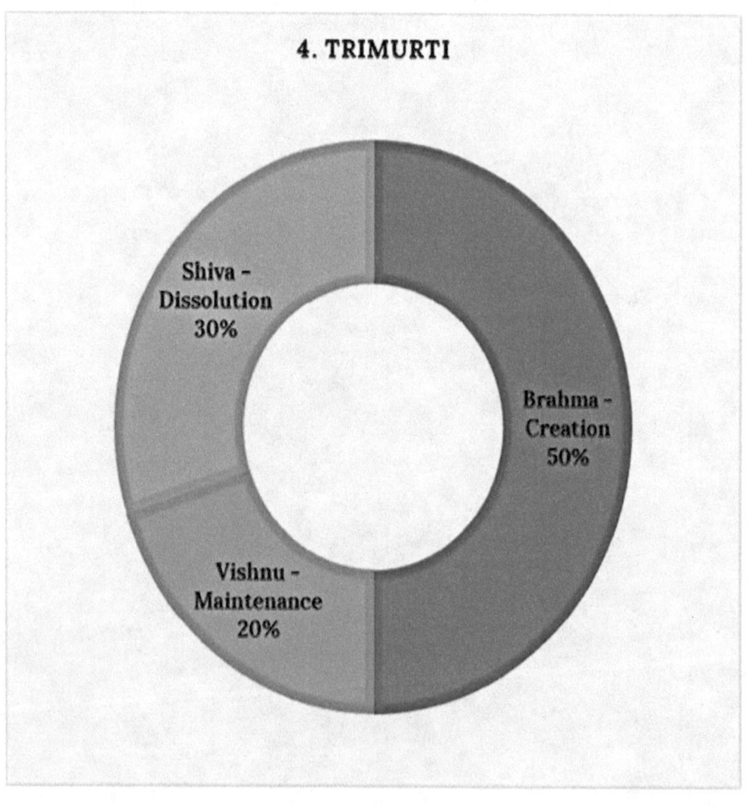

5. Gender	Male	Female	Neuter	Total
Count	5	4	1	10
Percentage	50%	40%	10%	100%

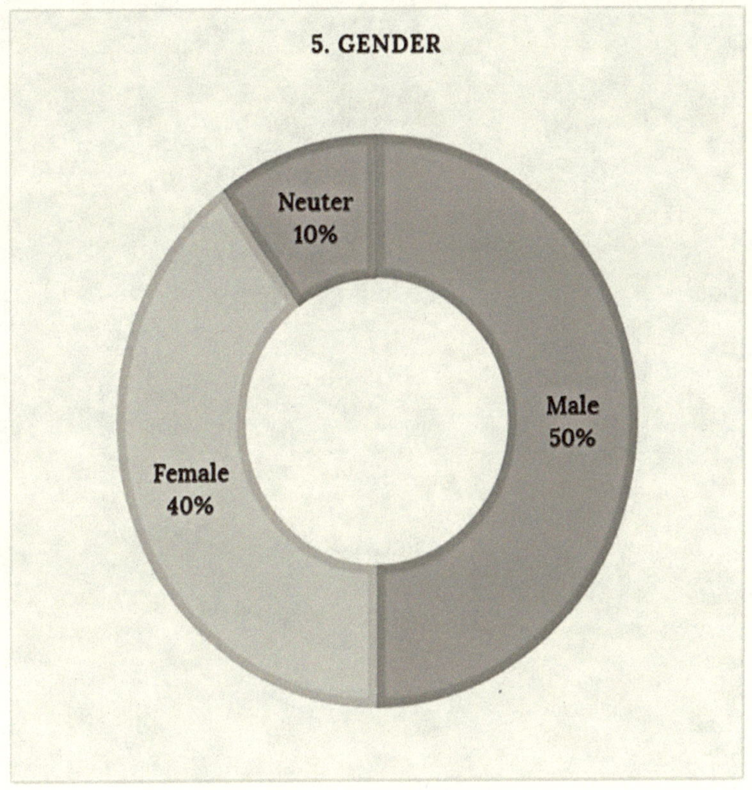

6. Gana	Deva	Manushya	Rakshasa	Total
Count	5	3	2	10
Percentage	50%	30%	20%	100%

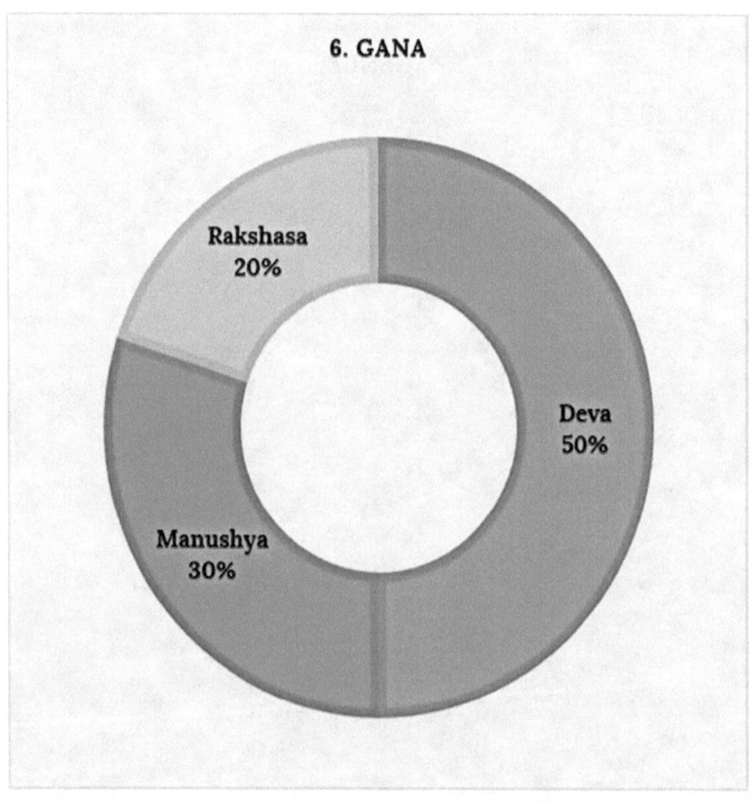

7. Guna	Satwic	Rajasic	Tamasic	Total
Count	3	5	2	10
Percentage	30%	**50%**	20%	100%

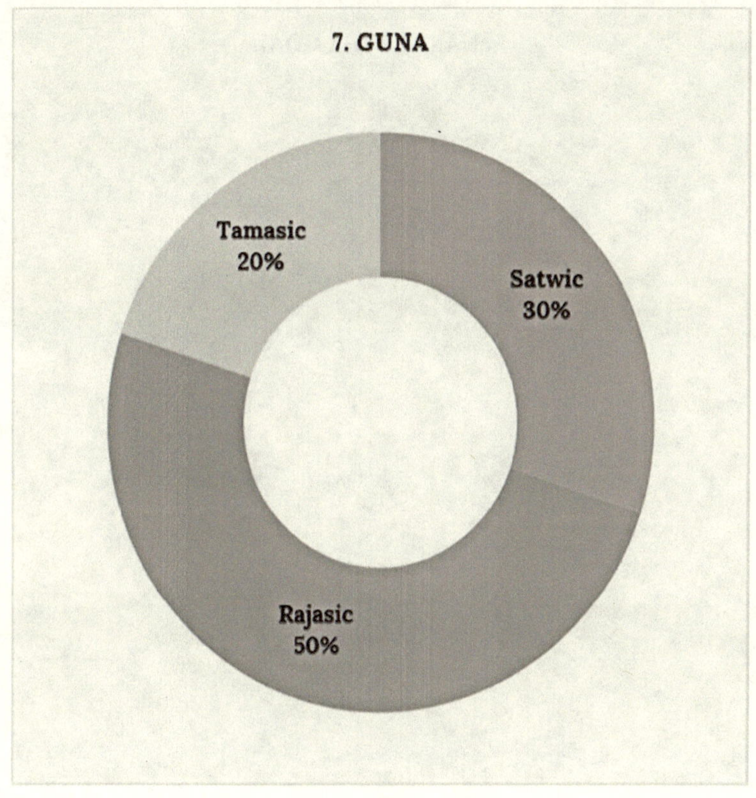

8. Nakshatra Goal	Dharma	Artha	Kama	Moksha	Total
Count	3	3	2	2	10
Percentage	30%	30%	20%	20%	100%

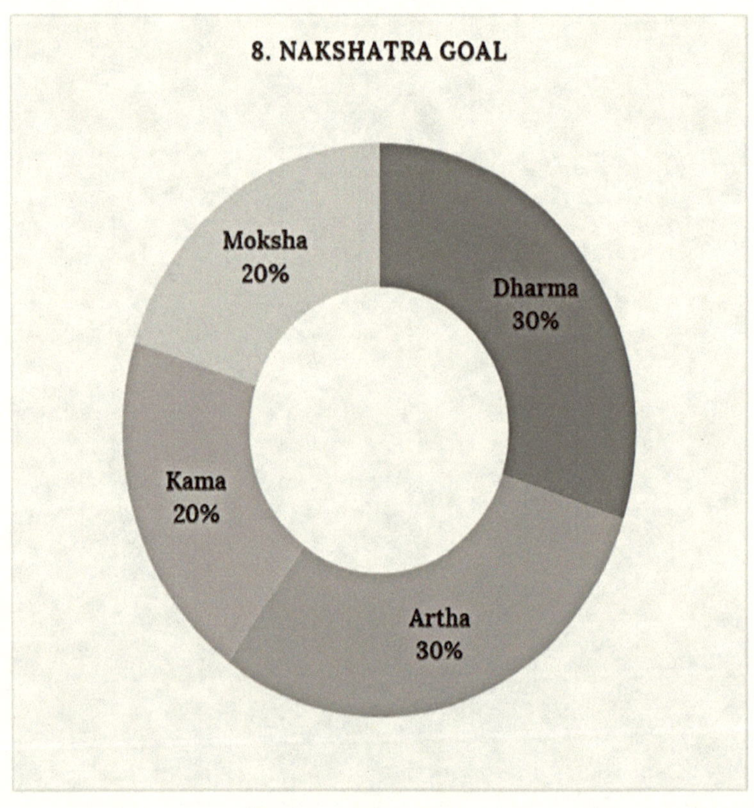

9. Pada Goal	Dharma	Artha	Kama	Moksha	Total
Count	1	2	3	4	10
Percentage	10%	20%	30%	**40%**	100%

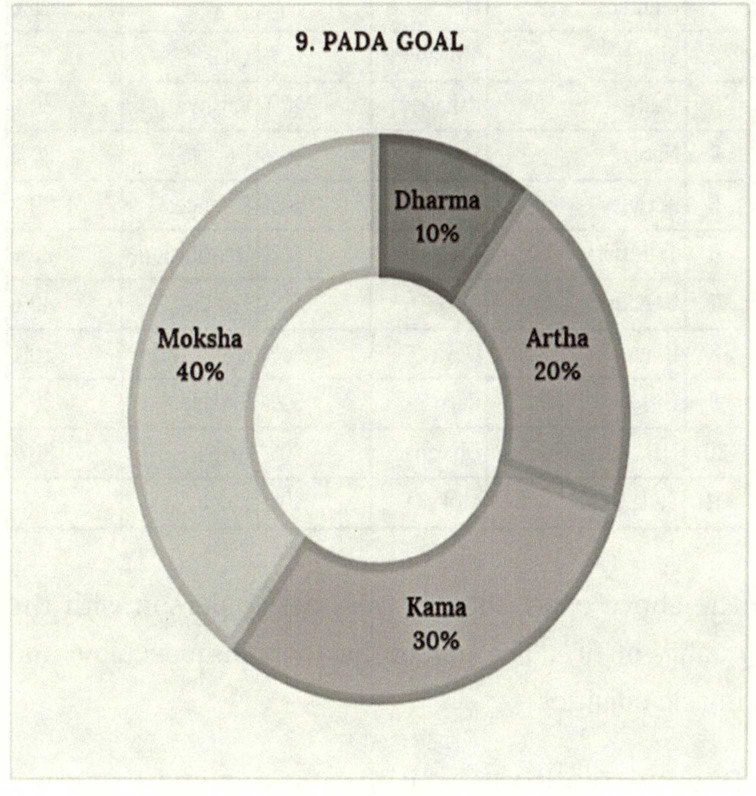

Conclusion:

No.	Quality	Quality -1		Quality -2	
1	Element	Fire	33%	Water	25%
2	Sign	Movable	67%	Dual	25%
3	Caste	Kshatriya	40%	Vaishya	30%
4	Nature	Swift	30%	Dhruva	30%
5	Activity	Passive	50%	Balanced	30%
6	TriMurti	Creation	50%	Dissolution	30%
7	Gender	Male	50%	Female	40%
8	Gana	Deva	50%	Manushya	30%
9	Guna	Rajasic	50%	Satwic	30%
10	Nakshatra Goal	Dharma	30%	Artha	30%
11	Pada Goal	Moksha	40%	Kama	30%

The above chart shows a very active person with the quality of fire. The person has benign, masculine and rajasic qualities.

Quality-1 indicates a fixed behavior and Quality-2 indicates subtle behaviors that are present in his personality but not visible under normal circumstances. These qualities come to the fore in special circumstances. Nakshatra goal indicates behavior in general circumstances and Pada goal indicates behavior in specific circumstances. Pada goal provides subtle information and whenever faced with the choice between Nakshatra goal and Pada goal, the person will choose the later.

Every person has many hidden qualities, this analysis can bring out all these hidden qualities and provide the necessary guidance in life.

Chapter 4

Friends and Enemies

❖ *Who is our friend and who is our enemy?*

We all meet different types of people in our life. Friends are those who are always ready to help and enemies are those who never help and are always ready to throw into the well. A very close friend and an enemy have a deep impact on our lives. Without true friends, it is very difficult for a person to move ahead in life and fight against odd circumstances. A friend can be anyone, someone from the family or someone outside the family can be a good friend, but the identity of a true friend is that he respects his friend and is always ready to help without any selfishness. The following few points provide the differences between these two;

- A friend always stands behind his friend to support him and prevent him from falling. The enemy also stands behind but is always ready to push.

- The friends who stand near us are called close friends and the enemies who stand around us are called close enemies.

- It is possible that a friend may fail to cooperate with you or may not answer your call when you need him, but the enemy never misses, they just wait for the opportunity, and the enemy is more alert than the friend.

People want to live among their friends and want to get rid of their enemies as soon as possible. The principle of friend and enemy not only works for humans but it also works on planets and stars.

With the help of the above description of friends and enemies, we will understand the principle of Shubh Kartari and Paap Kartari yoga that works not only in the birth chart but also in the transit of planets.

4.1 Shubh Kartari and Paap Kartari Yoga

Shubh Kartari Yoga is formed when a planet or a house is surrounded by benefic planets from both sides and Paap Kartari Yoga is formed when a planet or a house is surrounded by malefic planets on both sides without any beneficial aspect. This yoga can be understood better in a situation when both of our neighbors are good then they will help us, and when both of the neighbors are bad then no help will come, they will affect the matter of the house and create unnecessary problems. Sometimes the very presence of this kind of rogue person in their own house creates problems for their neighbours.

Shubh Kartari yoga increases the auspiciousness of the planet or house, while Paap Kartari yoga tends to cause difficulty for that planet or house. For example, let's say the Sun is in the first house, Saturn is in the second house, and Rahu is in the twelfth house. This planetary configuration in the horoscope forms a Papa Kartari Yoga, and in this case, the Sun is unable to give good results due to its hostile relationship with its neighboring planets. However, if Jupiter is in the second house and Mars is in the twelfth house, this combination gives rise to a Shubha Kartari Yoga, and the Sun's ability to give auspicious results is greatly enhanced.

4.2 Understand the Transit

When the natal Moon is surrounded or aspected by auspicious planets like Jupiter, Mercury, and Venus in transit, then it is the most auspicious time for the person. These planets support the person like a true friend and the pending work starts getting completed. The work which a person has been thinking about doing for years, now his true friends have come to help him and the tailwind starts in the life of the person.

Similarly, when the natal Moon is surrounded or aspected by malefic planets like Saturn, Rahu, and Ketu in transit, then obstacles start coming, it is like a car running smoothly on the road suddenly gets punctured.

Therefore, for predictions, it is necessary to see what kind of planets the natal Moon is surrounded by and what are the planets coming near it in transit. The planets transiting near the natal Moon are like close friends and enemies.

When the natal Moon is surrounded or aspected by benefic planets then positive things begin in the person's life and if it is surrounded by malefic planets then adversities begin in the person's life. The person who is close to us always has a deep impact whether he is a friend or an enemy. Similarly, the planet near the natal Moon has the power to have a deep impact on the life of a person.

When auspicious planets start coming near the natal Moon, things start changing in a person's life. It seems as if help has not arrived yet but information about the arrival of help has reached and this communication itself brings relief to the person.

It is important to identify those people in life who support us and also those who create enmity with us; we should get rid of these people as soon as possible. It takes a lot of time to recognize the true intentions of a person but astrology can help us identify those people with whom we can be connected for a long time and people whom we do not know but as soon as we meet, a feeling of estrangement immediately develop from them.

4.3 Yoni Koota Table

The Yoni Koota table provides adequate information about the characteristics of the individual, which is generally used in a very limited way in match making for the physical and mental compatibility of the bride and groom at the time of marriage. I found that Yoni Koota Table plays an important role in selection of our friends and enemies and if the Moon sign or Lagna of two persons matches each other then friendship starts immediately between them or vice versa.

Our ancient sages have assigned an animal to each Nakshatra and that animal immediately recognizes the animal hidden inside another person. If there is compatibility between the two then friendship starts and they like to live and help each other, if the animals are hostile towards each other then no relationship can flourish between them and enmity starts.

It doesn't matter how many years you've known the person, harmony can never develop if there is lack of animal compatibility. Each planet is located in a Nakshatra and has an animal assigned to each Nakshatra, so we must match compatibility not only with the ascendant and the Moon, but also with each planet and house.

(**Note:** *Readers may refer to my book "Animal Symbols of the Nakshatras" to know more about how animal behavior relates to humans.*)

Table - Animal Symbol and Inimical Yoni

Male	Female	Yoni Name	Inimical Yoni
Ashiwini	Satabhisha	Horse	Buffalo
Bharni	Revati	Elephant	Lion
Pushya	Krittika	Sheep (Goat)	Monkey
Rohini	Mrigashira	Serpent	Mongoose
Mula	Ardra	Dog	Deer
Aslesha	Punarvasu	Cat	Rat
Magha	Purva Phalguni	Rat	Cat
Uttara Phalguni	Uttara Bhadrapada	Bull / Cow	Tiger
Swati	Hasta	Buffalo	Horse
Vishakha	Chitra	Tiger	Cow
Jyeshtha	Anuradha	Deer (Hare)	Dog
Purva Ashadha	Shravana	Monkey	Sheep
Purva Bhadrapada	Dhanishta	Lion	Elephant
Uttara Ashadha		Mongoose	Serpent

Let's understand the whole concept with the example chart 1.

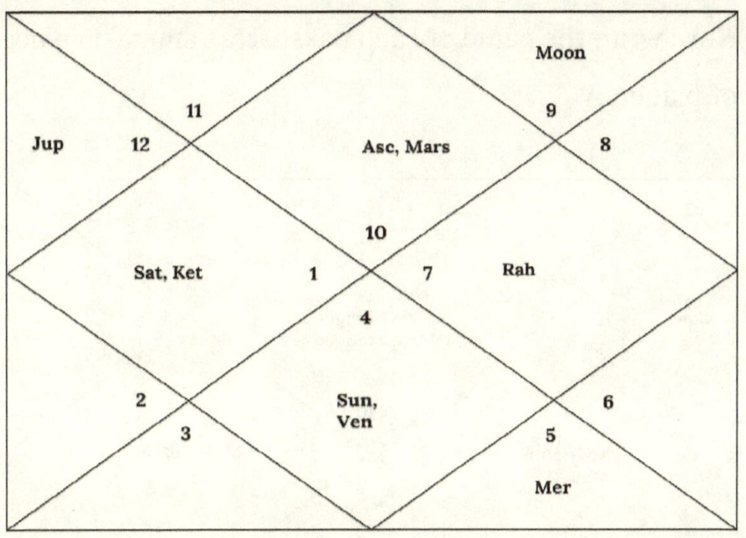

No.	Planets	Signs	Nakshatra	Animal
1	Asc.	Capricorn	Uttara Ashadha	Male Mongoose
2	Sun	Cancer	Pushya	Male Goat
3	Moon	Sagittarius	Mula	Male Dog
4	Mars (R)	Capricorn	U. Ashadha	Male Mongoose
5	Mercury (R)	Leo	Magha	Male Rat
6	Jupiter	Pisces	U. Bhadrapada	Cow
7	Venus	Cancer	Pururvasu	Female Cat
8	Saturn	Aries	Ashwini	Male Horse
9	Rahu (R)	Libra	Swati	Male Buffalo
10	Ketu (R)	Aries	Ashwini	Male Horse

Now, write the name of each nakshatra's animal in place of planets.

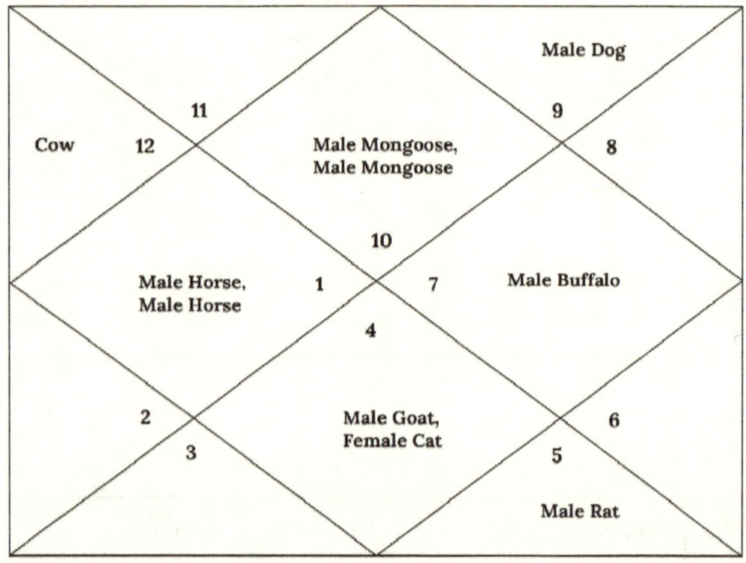

Now we can see the influence of animal in the personality of the person. The animal of one person immediately identifies the animal of the other person. That is the reason when we meet a new person likes and dislikes start automatically developing with us. In which Nakshatra the Moon is placed the animal of that Nakshatra is very important because Moon represents our mind.

The next is the ascendant; the animal of ascendant is the next important animal because ascendant represents our physical stature. At first, we have to analyze the compatibility of the animal of the Moon sign between the two persons.

In the example chart 1, the animal of Moon is a male dog, hence this person can easily make a friendship when he will meet a person of any male or female dog nakshatra, it means, a person whose moon is placed in Mula or Ardra nakshatra, harmony automatically start between the two.

Every gender immediately recognizes its opposite gender and friendship and intimacy develops. A male dog indicates that friendship quickly start when he will meet with a female dog, that means a person whose Moon is placed in Ardra nakshatra then the friendship continues between the two and both of them like the company of each other. The same principle we can apply with the ascendant and check its compatibility with ascendant and Moon of the other person.

In this case, the ascendant is placed in Uttara Ashadha Nakshatra, whose animal is the male mongoose and no counterpart has been given to this Nakshatra by our ancient sages.

Uttara Ashadha also indicates friendship with Muslims or foreigners and when the dasha or antardasha of the planet placed in Uttara Ashadha (Mars) starts at a certain age, then there is a possibility of entry of a Muslim or foreigner in the life of the person, who provides good support. When a male animal meets its female counterpart, the relationship between the two individuals lasts for a long time; they are always ready to help each other.

The reverse of the above sentence is also true with the inimical yoni. In the example chart, dog inimical yoni is deer and the nakshatra of deer is Jyeshta and Anuradha. If a person Moon sign is placed in Jyeshta or Anuradha nakshatra then both of them can't sit together and a feeling of disharmony automatically develops between the two.

No matter whether they are husband and wife, employer or employee, father or son etc. I have observed that when the Moon signs of both are in inimical yoni, there is no compatibility between the two persons.

The information of Yoni is very useful at the work place too. If an employee and a boss both have inimical yoni, then both of them don't like each other. Employee will not get any recognition of his hard work and this will hamper his career and vice versa.

In the example chart, at his work place the person he will make friendship with; Dog, Mongoose and Buffalo person. It means the person will make friendship with Mula, Ardra, Uttara Ashadha, Swati and Hasta nakshatra people.

The information of Yoni is not only limited to identify our friends and foes. It is very useful to identify the synchronicity between body and mind of the same person. The animal of the mind supports the animal of the body, only then the body accepts the order of the mind and swiftness is visible in the personality of these people.

For example, if Moon is placed in Mula nakshatra and ascendant is placed is Ardra nakshatra then mind and body work together and the person is very quick. These people perform excellent in those jobs where proper synchronicity of body and mind is required.

If a person Moon is placed in Pushya nakshatra and his ascendant is in Krittika nakshatra, then there is a strong synergy between his mind and body and the person excels in his field. Famous football player Pele's Moon is in Pushya and ascendant is in Krittika and he in known as legend of football.

The placement of inimical animal of mind and body create confusion and the person is unable to take proper decision because whatever the mind says his body immediately rejects that order and what the body does mind doesn't support them. Such people are always in dilemma and are unable to take appropriate and timely decisions.

Chapter 5

Atmakaraka
and
Karakamsha

5.1 Karakas in Jaimini Astrology

According to Jaimini astrology, the karaka is of great importance and it varies for each horoscope. Karaka means factor, significator or agent. The determination of the karaka is based on the longitude of the planet from the beginning of the respective sign. Following are the seven main karakas;

i) Atmakaraka - This is the planet having the highest longitude in a sign. The strength of this planet reflects the general strength of the horoscope. The natural Atmakaraka is considered the Sun. For example; suppose among all planets the Moon has the highest longitude is 27 degrees in Aries. So, Moon is considered as an Atmakaraka in this horoscope.

ii) Amatya karaka - The planet in a sign having the second-highest longitude becomes the Amatya karaka. There is no natural Amatya karaka but Mercury is considered for the same.

iii) Bhratru karaka - The planet in a sign having the third-highest longitude becomes the Bhratru karaka. It rules over the events pertaining to our siblings. Mars is considered a natural Bhratru karaka.

iv) Matru karaka - The fourth planet in order of longitude becomes Matru karaka. Moon (is considered as Mother) is the natural Matru karaka.

v) Putra karaka - The fifth planet in order of longitude becomes Putra karaka. It is considered the lord of children and Jupiter is the natural significator for this karaka.

vi) Gnati karaka - The next planet in order of degree becomes Gnati karaka. It is considered the lord of relations and Mars is considered as natural significator of this karaka.

vii) Dara karaka - The planet least in order of degree becomes Dara karaka, an indicator of spouse, marriage, and partnership. Venus is the natural significator of Dara karaka.

While determining the karaka do not multiply with the longitude of the sign, consider only the position of the planet in a sign up to a degree, minutes and seconds.

5.2 Atmakaraka: A New Perspective

Sun represents soul, and every soul has done various good and bad deeds and the responsibility of all of them comes in this life. The imprint of all those deeds is present on the soul and the Atmakaraka planet represents it.

There is a definite purpose for a planet to be an Atmakaraka planet. It indicates that the soul has done various karmas (deeds) related to that planet, hence, it is the most karmic planet and the person is responsible for all his karmas. The Atmakaraka planet experiences the maximum amount of karma, the incomplete obligations of the person become a burden and every person has to bear the burden of his karma. It is the continuation of journey which we left in our past birth. Hence, the information about these seven karakas provides useful information about the person and among them Atmakaraka is the most important and is considered as the King.

A strong king is required to run a kingdom and he is surrounded by a good team of advisors. Therefore, an Atmakaraka planet should be strong in the horoscope and receive positive aspect of his supporting planets. A weak and poorly placed Atmakaraka indicates that the native is unable to take decisions and aspect of malefic planets create hamper in life.

It is important to consider in which Nakshatra the Atmakaraka is placed, because, the journey of this life will start from where it was left in the previous life. If the Atmakaraka is placed at Gandanta, it means that a new beginning in this life is waiting for the person, a new beginning can be either good or bad. It can push a person into a deep abyss or give them the opportunity to take a huge leap forward in life. Therefore, one should always perform good deeds. Because Gandanta is a boiling point and the planet feels highly uncomfortable at this place. Neither a person nor the planet wants to stay at the boiling point.

Mahadev Pathaka in Jataka Tatva has written (T-36) that during the Bhukti of Atmakaraka planet, the person falls from his position and there is a possibility of loss.

5.3 Why are Rahu and Ketu not considered Atmakaraka?

Rahu indicates selfish activities and Ketu indicates selfless activities. Rahu represents worldly pursuits and denial of spirituality and Ketu represents spiritual inclination and denial of material world.

Atmakaraka planet indicates burning of karmic burdens, if Rahu become Atmakaraka then karmas will never burn because Rahu is complete darkness and salvation will be impossible for eternal. Ketu indicates salvation, means no bondage of material world, therefore, author support the opinion that Rahu and Ketu can't become Atmakaraka.

5.4 Qualities of Atmakaraka

Before making any decision, it is necessary to identify the Atmakaraka planet in the horoscope because it plays an important role in the decision taken by the person. Following are some of the qualities of a planet when it is Atmakaraka.

1. Sun: The native has leadership abilities and the courage to walk alone on unknown paths. Such natives are creative and have the ability to take risks, but this also makes the person arrogant. Such a person becomes proud of his position and wealth. Arrogance creates heat and heat gives birth to separation. Therefore, these people should learn humility in life.

2. Moon: The native is receptive and compassionate. Moon is considered a mother, so the native has caring qualities. Strong Moon indicates the power of imagination and the person can excel in those works where such skills are required.

3. Mars: Such a person is courageous, passionate, and adventurous by nature. The planet of war and weapons does not think twice before taking any steps. Therefore, such a person should avoid all kinds of violence. Yoga, spiritual development, and martial arts also require the energy of Mars. Consequently, they should use such energy only for creative purposes.

4. Mercury: The native is strong in communication and networking. He is an intelligent person, has many friends, and is good at writing and editing. He is adaptable, witty, and diplomatic.

5. Jupiter: The native is a very knowledgeable person. He takes an interest in religious activities and is skilled in giving advice. He is a truthful and honest person and is respected as a Guru or Head.

6. Venus: The native is interested in art and music, and likes cleanliness everywhere. Being a female planet, the native represents feminine qualities and shows manners and etiquette in life.

7. Saturn: The native is very hardworking, honest and just. He is a responsible and disciplined person but has to face many challenges in life.

5.5 Result of Atmakaraka in Navamsha Position

Following are the results of Atmakaraka planet occupies various signs in Navamsha as per Jaimini Sutras (Adhyaya - 1, Pada - 2);

1. When Atmakaraka occupies Aries Navamsha then the person will be prey to fear and bites of rats, cats and other similar animals.

2. When Atmakaraka occupies Taurus Navamsha then there will be trouble or happiness from quadrupeds. **Note:** The meaning of quadrupeds is old days are cows, horses, bulls, etc. But nowadays we can relate it to four-wheelers. If Atmakaraka is weak in the natal chart then it will create trouble and if Atmakaraka is strong in the natal chart then it creates happiness.

3. When Atmakaraka occupies Gemini Navamsha then the person suffers from obesity, itching and skin related boils.

4. When Atmakaraka occupies Cancer Navamsha then troubles from watery places and leprosy.

Note: The sutra indicates that using dirty water can cause water-related diseases or make the person afraid of going near water.

5. When Atmakaraka occupies Leo Navamsha then danger will come from dogs and other such canines.

Note: The sutra indicates that trouble or diseases comes from foxes, wolves, jackals, and other members of the dog family.

6. When Atmakaraka occupies Virgo Navamsha then the person will suffer from fire, itching and obesity.

7. When Atmakaraka occupies Libra Navamsha then the person will earn a lot of money from business.

8. When Atmakaraka occupies Scorpio Navamsha then the person is afraid of aquatic animals and reptiles and does not even get milk from his mother.

9. When Atmakaraka occupies Sagittarius Navamsha, then the person faces danger from falling from a high place, from vehicle, etc., and from places like trees, mountains etc.

10. When Atmakaraka occupies Capricorn Navamsha then the person will suffer from aquatic animals, fierce birds, skin problem, large wounds and enlargement of glands.

11. When Atmakaraka occupies Aquarius Navamsha, then the person will take interest in charitable works and construct wells, tanks, gardens, temples, and rest houses for pilgrims.

Note: The sutra indicates that the person will perform philanthropic work for the public at large.

12. When Atmakaraka occupies Pisces Navamsha, that person will be a highly religious person, will perform religious activities and will attain final emancipation.

Note: The sutra indicate that the person will take interest in cultural and religious activities and spread knowledge.

The placement of Atmakaraka in Navamsha is very important. If its position is beneficial in Navamsha and receives aspect of beneficial planets then the person lives a happy and prosperous life. A badly placed Atmakaraka indicates troubles and the person lives a miserable life.

5.6 Atmakaraka with other Planets in Navamsha

Atmakaraka planet influenced by the planet placed in the same sign. Jaimini Sutras further explains the result of Atmakaraka with other Planets in Navamsha.

1. Atmakaraka with the Sun – The person will work in government service and political activities.

Note: Sun indicates government and if Sun is Atmakaraka or is related to Atmakaraka Sun then it indicates the native's involvement in government work or activities.

2. Atmakaraka with Full Moon and Venus – The person will live a comfortable life with luxuries and will work as an educationist by profession.

Note: Strength of Moon indicates strength of mind and full moon indicates a person with stable mind and Venus bestows the person with luxuries.

3. Atmakaraka with Mars – The native works as a metalist and possesses expertise in arms, weapons and products related with metal. He will do a profession related with fire, chemical and drugs.

Note: Work related with heat and fire can be seen here, like engine drivers, cooks and weapon makers who prepare various chemicals to change the quality of metal.

4. Atmakaraka with Mercury – The native work as a trader, businessman, weaver or sculptor. Such a person is gentle in behavior and proficient in social activities.

Note: Mercury provides business acumen to the person and a strong Atmakaraka indicates strong understanding for business.

5. Atmakaraka with Jupiter – The native takes deep interest in religious activities. He is a righteous, knowledgeable, person and well versed in Vedas and scriptures.

Note: Jupiter indicates knowledge and wisdom, and association of Atmakaraka indicates that the planet bestows the person with such qualities.

6. Atmakaraka with Venus – Such a person is a political figure or works as a government official. He is a passionate person, loves many women and lives for 100 years.

Note: Venus represents the desire for sexual pleasure and this passion remains in the person for a long time.

7. Atmakaraka with Saturn – Saturn gives success in the chosen activity and as a result the person becomes famous.

Note: The fame given by Rahu does not last long but the fame given by Saturn lasts for ages. Saturn indicates struggle; hence the person will achieve success after a lot of struggle. Saturn elevates the person to a higher position and bestows success and fame.

8. Atmakaraka with Rahu – Such a person produces bows and arrows. He earns his livelihood by stealing or deceiving. He deals with poisons and dangerous chemicals. He works in the field of medicine and is excellent in the work of iron and steel and other manufacturing industries.

Note: Rahu indicates work related to big machinery. Such a person can easily handle large machinery and other equipment related to iron and steel. Bows and arrows indicate guns, bullets and other warlike instruments. Stealing means that he is skilled in doing work without others knowing and deceiving indicates use of malpractices in the related work.

9. Atmakaraka with Ketu – Such a person earns his livelihood with or through elephants, he may be a thief.

Note: Elephant is a peaceful animal, it indicates silently engage in doing a big task and a thief indicates act of doing such things without being notice of others. Association with Ketu indicates a person who silently engages in his activities and don't like to be noticed by others.

5.7 Karakamsha

Where the Atmakaraka planet is situated in Navamsha, that zodiac sign is called Karakamsha. Wherever the lord of Karakamsha is situated in the natal horoscope that zodiac sign is made the ascendant of the Karakamsha horoscope and the remaining planets change their houses accordingly.

For example; In D1 chart, suppose the planet with the highest longitudinal degree is Moon. Find the position of Moon in D9 chart; suppose it is placed in Gemini, then Gemini is called Karakamsha.

To prepare Karakamsha chart, find in which sign the lord of Gemini i.e. Mercury is situated in D1 chart, suppose it is situated in Sagittarius, make Sagittarius the Karakamsha ascendant and move the rest of the planets.

Atmakaraka planet is the karaka of soul, hence Karakamsha chart tells more about the soul and the individual.

Chapter 6

Planetary Strengths and Weaknesses

Before starting predictions, it is necessary to observe the strengths and weaknesses of the planets. There are many methods to identify the strength and weakness of a planet. Following are some important points to check which I have already written in my book "Vedic Astrology: Light of Wisdom". Here, I will discuss its meaning;

6.1 Strength of Planets Based on Its Degrees

While observing the chart it is necessary to observe the degree of the planets. A planet in the first or last two degree of a zodiac sign is considered to be powerless and does not give good results to the houses ruled by it.

Various states of Planets as per its degree -

- Adolescence Planet– Between 2° to 10°

- Young Planet – Between 10° to 22°

- Old Planet – Between 22° to 28°

- Dead Planet – Between 28° to 30° and 0° to 2°

Adolescence Planet: At Adolescence age, people begin to learn about the world, they spend a lot of time in each other's company or communicating on phone or chatting on internet. But at this age people lack experience and looks for direction from senior members. Therefore, it is the best time to gather knowledge.

A planet between 2° to 10° indicates immaturity of the person. It indicates that such a person is unable to take wise decisions in life.

Young Planet: When a person becomes young he is vigorous, lively and full with energy. Similarly, when a planet is situated between 10° to 22°, it gives maximum results. These results can be positive or negative and depend on other combinations.

Old Planet: At this age, a person attains sufficient maturity and is well aware of common mistakes. With his experience he has the ability to provide guidance to newcomers.

Similarly, when a planet is situated between 22° to 28° then it is considered to be a very mature planet and is strong enough to take necessary decisions. Such a person learns quickly in life, behave in a matured manner and able to provide guidance to others.

Dead Planet: Ancient texts says that when a planet is placed between 28° to 30° and 0° to 2° it is considered as dead planet. I have seen that many people take these two positions blindly, but there is a difference between them.

A planet between 0° to 2° should be considered as a newborn baby. A baby is dependent for its existence on others, it feels panic quickly and looks for support. Similarly, when a planet is between 0° to 2°, it is like a newborn baby who needs support for others, such a person gets nervous quickly in adverse situations and looks for a safe place like a child.

When a planet is placed between 28° to 30°, it is also considered a dead planet. Like a 90 years old person who is on bed but the person has seen the world. He has seen that when and how the tide turns, he has seen the changing faces of his near ones. He is a very experienced and mature person but lacks energy. A planet at these degrees should not be considered as the planet situated at 0° to 2° but it should be considered as enough mature and highly experienced planet.

But there is a drawback to this placement. Like the ego of an old person, the planets placed on these degrees indicate the stubborn and rigid nature of the person. Such people think that they are always right and they never change their decision under any circumstances. They always try to protect their ego.

6.2 Maran Karaka Sthana

Some places in the horoscope are not suitable for planets because that place is against the tendency of that planet and they feel uncomfortable just by sitting there. We also do not like to sit in some places and many times we refuse to sit there, but what happens when we have to sit there forcefully, our whole mind gets disturbed. Similarly, the planets located at the Maran Karaka place also do not work properly and create disturbance in the life of the native.

6.2.1 Sun: The 12th house is the Maran Karaka Sthana

This is the house of illusion, dreams, sleep, subconscious mind, hidden fears, retreat from the external world, etc. Sun means activity, go away from bed, no illusion, no darkness and no fear. The quality of this house does not support the qualities of the Sun and the planet feels highly uncomfortable at this place.

Sun in the 12th house indicates lack of sleep, this means these people are perfectly suited for jobs where night duty is involved.

6.2.2 Moon: The 8th house is the Maran Karaka Sthana

Moon is very sensitive and soft planet and represents our mind and emotions. The 8th house indicates death and hidden activities of the person. The nature of the 8th house doesn't fit the qualities of the Moon and the planet feels highly uncomfortable in this house.

The 8th house Moon indicates a restless person who takes interest in solving mysteries and questions continuously rotates in his mind, no matter how many years has gone, until he finds the truth the search is on. Such a person never feels satisfied do to one type of job during his whole life. Being a restless person, he changes many jobs in his life or his life force him for change. They have natural inclination for philosophy, psychology, occult and other hidden things in life.

They do not take interest on superficial things and are always involve searching those things that is not easily visible. To perform all these tasks, it is necessary for the Moon to be strong in the eighth house, otherwise the person quickly gets nervous and falls into depression.

6.2.3 Mars: The 7th house is the Maran Karaka Sthana

The 7th house is the house of marriage and partnership and Mars represents celibacy. Mars is the planet of dominance and aggression and this quality doesn't fit with the qualities of the 7th house. The functioning of the 7th house is totally different with the temperament of Mars. The energy of the planet force to take initiative but environment doesn't support, so what to do under these circumstances.

Mars is a bachelor planet; hence, Mars in 7th house indicates late marriage or living alone after marriage.

6.2.4 Mercury: The 7th house is the Maran Karaka Sthana

Mercury is considered as child and 7th house is the house of marriage. The 7th house is the house of intimacy with the partner and soft feelings. There is no logic in songs and poetry, in the matter of emotions feeling of heart is important and Mercury indicates logic and conclusion.

Mercury in 7th house indicates such a person seeks logic in their romantic discussion, therefore, he lacks the quality of romance. Such a person doesn't like romantic movies and lovable songs, etc. because he looks for logics and justifications in these matters also.

6.2.5 Jupiter: The 3rd house is the Marana Karaka Sthana

Jupiter, the planet of wisdom, does not like to sit in a place where there is a lot of physical activity. The third house is the house of courage and aggression and Jupiter is the planet of peace and spirituality, therefore, Jupiter feels uncomfortable in this house.

When a planet feels uncomfortable it becomes unable to provide its natural qualities to the person. The quality of Jupiter is to provide direction, in the third house indicates that such a person takes wrong decisions.

6.2.6 Venus: The 6th house is the Maran Karaka Sthana

Venus is a planet of love and sensuality, these are tender qualities and the 6th house indicates struggle and competition. It is the house of celibacy, bachelor life, discipline, competition and fight. These qualities are far away from the qualities of Venus. Hence, the planet of love feels highly uncomfortable in the 6th house.

Venus in the sixth house indicates that the person will be looking for love and support but will lack it in his/her life. Circumstances in his life will ruthlessly destroy his tender qualities.

6.2.7 Saturn: The 1st house is the Maran Karaka Sthana

First house indicates physical stature, health and appearance in general. The significator of the first house is Sun, which denotes health, energy and vigor. Saturn is a slow-moving planet, significator of disease and death, Saturn puts brakes on the speed and teaches the person to have control over things.

The quality of Saturn is completely different from the quality of the first house and the planet of justice fails to give good results here. Such a person becomes a lethargic person and he doesn't like to move from the place where he sits even after shouting from other members of the family.

Saturn put the person into isolation, therefore, these people prefer their lonely life and don't want to mingle with others.

6.2.8 Rahu: The 9th house is the Marana Karaka Sthana

The 9th house represents religion and spirituality and Rahu is away from all types of religious activities. Rahu – the planet of deceit and cheating doesn't like to follow the path of truth and wisdom.

Rahu in 9th house indicates that such a person doesn't like to go to temple and believe in religion. He always thinks about how to increase profits and he builds relationships only with those people from where some profit is possible. People who have Rahu in the ninth house stay far away from religion or religion is just a business for them.

6.3 Yog-Karaka

The word Yog-Karaka comes from the two words; "Yog" means addition or conjunction or union and Karaka means significator. Yog-karaka defines a situation when a planet possesses both Kendra (1, 4, 7, and 10) and Trikona (1, 5, and 9) house from any ascendant without owning the Dusthana houses (6th, 8th, and 12th).

Such planet gets unique property as Kendra and Trikona houses are considered strong houses. Occupancy of two strong houses by the same planet indicates good coordination between those houses and that planet is completely responsible for all matters related to it.

If the Yog-Karaka planet is exalted, situated in his own sign or in a friendly sign then such a planet provides excellent results in its dasha and antardasha. Retrograde or combust Yog-Karaka planet should not be considered bad, they also have the potential to provide to provide fruitful results when the time comes.

Yog-Karaka planet uplift the strength of the horoscope and also protect the person from negativities in life because there is a positive energy present all the time related to that houses and this harmony produces rhythm in life.

We can assume that the Yoga-karaka planet is a very energetic planet and its efficiency is higher as compared to other planets.

Only three planets; Saturn, Mars and Venus act as Yog-Karaka planets. For different ascendants the Yog-Karaka planets are;

i. Taurus: Saturn - 9th and 10th lord

ii. Cancer: Mars - 5th and 10th lord

iii. Leo: Mars - 4th and 9th lord

iv. Libra: Saturn - 4th and 5th lord

v. Capricorn: Venus - 5th and 10th lord

vi. Aquarius: Venus - 4th and 9th lord

When Saturn becomes Yog-Karaka it brings discipline in life, tests patience and provides long-term success to the person.

When Mars becomes Yog-Karaka it creates energy and enthusiasm in the person, such a person is brave, fights injustice and achieves success with his courage.

When Venus becomes Yog-Karaka, it enhances the artistic qualities of the person. The person has a natural inclination towards the qualities of Venus and the lord of the love provides financial prosperity to the person.

6.4 Vargottama Planet

When a planet is in the same sign in the birth chart and the Navamsha chart, then that planet is called Vargottama planet. It is made up of two words 'Varga' and 'Uttama'. Vargottama means that the planet has become very powerful in the horoscope of the person.

Whenever a planet is Vargottama, the qualities of that planet become a part of the person's characteristics. Locating a planet in the same sign as D1 and D9 chart is the primary role in finding Vargottama planet. A badly placed planet in Vargottama means it can give more bad results.

Every planet has its own strength and weaknesses and it is important to consider the Navamsha chart along with the natal chart. The ninth house represents the fortune of the person and Navamsha chart is the expansion of the ninth house.

Correct predictions cannot be made just by looking at the D1 chart, every person's fortune pulls him, and therefore, it is necessary to observe the position of the planets in the Navamsha chart. A strong planet in Navamsha chart indicates that the fortune of the person is strong. Occupying the same zodiac sign in both charts means that the energy of the planet is well integrated, which means that there is continuity in such energy. When there are no obstacles, the results will be easily available.

While analyzing the horoscope we should also analyze the zodiac changes in D1 and D9 charts. Suppose a planet is debilitated in D1 chart and exalted in D9 chart or vice versa.

In both the situations, there is a change in the energy of the planet and the person has to go through such changes in his life. When the energy level changes then life does not remain smooth and stable and the events related to that planet and house take their shape when the dasha or antardasha of that planet comes.

6.5 Mutual Exchange of Signs

When two planets occupy each other's signs, they are said to be in exchange or parivartan. This is a very powerful condition and will greatly enhance the houses the planets occupy as well as the houses the planets rule. In this exchange the affairs of two houses work together.

It's like two people living in each other's house. Therefore, both of them stay in harmony with each other and take care of the matters related to the house because both of them know very well that any kind of disturbance in this house can worsen the matters at my house. Therefore, the energy in mutual exchange works for coordination and enriches both the houses.

Parivartan should not be limited only for exchange of signs; it includes Nakshatra, Karaka and Navamsha as well. In Parivartan Yoga, enemy planets are also unable to produce their negative results.

Chapter 7

Transit of Planets

A horoscope is a snapshot of the sky when a person is born, the zodiac signs that rise and set at the time and the planetary positions in them, guide the life path of the person. But the planets are not fixed, they keep on moving and transiting through different signs. This transit produces different types of energy. Although the effect of the transiting planet is temporary in our life and when the planet moves out of the zodiac, the energy level changes, and then its effect also changes.

We can understand the planets in the birth chart as mother and father, who always have an impact on us, no matter how old we become. The transiting planet is like our class teacher, when we study in class 1st then our class teacher has full right to punish us, but when we leave the class and study in higher classes, then the authority goes to that class teacher. Similarly, the transiting planet affects us as long as it remains in that sign. When it leaves and some other planet comes then the right to influence us goes to the newcomer. But what we got from our parents affects our whole life, in the same way; the planets of birth affect us throughout life.

Transit provides us with useful information about upcoming changes in energy levels and favorable and unfavorable times. The information guides us to channelize our energy in the right direction, make better use of available resources, and take necessary measures on gloomy days. This information also destroys the person's ego and despair, that there is higher energy working behind us, as a human we only have to do our work, and "I did" the attachment to the word disappears. We have to sow only good seeds, fruits will come when the time turns favourable.

The effect of transits of slow-moving planets – Jupiter, Saturn, Rahu and Ketu are longer than that of fast-moving planets. Jupiter stays in a sign for almost a year, Saturn stays in a sign for 2.5 years, Rahu and Ketu stay in a sign for 1.5 years. Many life changing events take place during this transit which affects the person deeply.

Jupiter, Venus, unafflicted Mercury, and Moon (more than 72 degrees) are considered benefic planets. While transiting they produce favorable results when they conjoin or make aspects with the position of planets in our natal chart. Sun is considered kroora (cruel) and Mars, Saturn, Rahu, and Ketu are considered malefic and produce unfavorable results when they conjoin or make aspects with the planets in our horoscope. When a benefic planet transits in its favourable signs and conjoins or makes an aspect with a benefic planet then it produces favorable results and vice-versa.

Jupiter's most favorable sign is cancer, therefore, when Jupiter transit through cancer most favorable results is possible, while Saturn's most detrimental sign is also cancer, when Saturn transits into Cancer many life-changing events happen.

7.1 The Transit of Jupiter

Jupiter takes about a year time to cross a sign and complete the entire zodiac in 11.9 years. Therefore, after every 12 years, Jupiter transits over its natal Jupiter, and that time brings remarkable changes in the life of the person. Jupiter is the most benefic planet, so its transit brings luck, happiness, and success in life. When Jupiter transits over the natal Moon or 7th house or makes an aspect then most of the native's marriages happen at that time. It bestows the person with children, wealth, and happy life. One of the most auspicious times comes when it transits the 2nd, 5th, 7th, 9th, and 11th houses from the natal Moon.

When all the hopes and aspirations of a person fail and he is about to fall into the pit of despair, Jupiter helps at the last moment. Therefore, the transit of Jupiter and its aspect is very significant as it brings many life changing events and the lamp of hope gets lit again in the life of person.

(**Note:** *For detailed explanation of Jupiter, readers can refer to my book, "Jupiter: The Planet of Fortune".*)

7.2 The Transit of Saturn

Saturn completes its cycle in 29.5 years and stays in a sign for 2.5 years. The tough master transit brings limitations, restrictions, delays, and misfortunes. When Saturn transits over the natal Sun, problems with the father, seniors, and authorities are possible. Saturn is the challenger, so subordinate will challenge their superiors and the transit creates a lot of trouble in the native's life.

Saturn's transit over Moon brings problems with mother, depression, and mental agony. Saturn transit over Venus brings trouble with the wife, female relatives, and scandals. Its transit over Mars brings quarrels and accidents, its transit over Jupiter brings financial gains and the start of a new venture, success in investments; its transit over Mercury brings trouble through documents, also increased interest in literature and study. Saturn's transit over natal Saturn brings significant changes in life and it put questions on everything that the person has done till now is his life.

Saturn means balance and discipline. The transit of Saturn teaches the person to be balanced, it destroys the ego of the person and shows the real truth of life. Saturn acts as a cleaner and cleans everything that has become garbage in our lives. People get attached to their garbage and are not ready to remove it from their lives.

When garbage accumulates on the road and the cleaner does not come, then after a few days it becomes impossible to walk on the roads. The working style of Saturn is also similar to that of the garbage cleaner. When garbage accumulates everywhere, life becomes difficult, diseases start spreading, and progress stops. Therefore, for development, it is necessary to remove the garbage first. Development cannot happen without removing the garbage, whether it is a house or a city.

The same principle applies to every person's life as well. Without removing the garbage, no one can move forward in life, and due to our ignorance, pebbles and garbage get collected, so cleanliness is necessary for development. Saturn is harsh and shows no mercy when the question of removal of waste comes, without which there is no growth. Therefore, the ancient sutra (Sthan Vridhi Karo Shani) is right about Saturn that where it is placed, it increases the results of that place by removing all the dirt of that place.

The position of Saturn in a horoscope indicates that there is a lot of growth potential, but hard work is required. Saturn never gives any fruit without any hard work. The position of Saturn also indicates that we should be ready to work hard as there are many obstacles to overcome. Therefore, the transit of Saturn plays an important role in life. Saturn removes every adulteration, every falsehood, and every garbage then only the truth remains. Saturn throws every unnecessary thing in life. Hence, it is said that Saturn shows the real truth to the person by cleaning every dirt.

Today, this human body which is liked by many people, a day will come when no one will like it. One day it will turn into waste and people will throw it in the crematorium and burn it like garbage. When Saturn transits on the ascendant it gives disease, it means that some part of the body has become waste and taken by Saturn and one day the whole body will become waste. Every waste has to be thrown away, but people get attached to their waste and do not want to remove it. They keep collecting it for years, but they do not know that it has become a burden for their development.

Saturn throws away all the garbage and if the person is not ready to leave it then He has to use force. So, Saturn is harsh because it does not allow any kind of garbage to be kept in our lives. When Sade Sati starts people start getting scared because they are not ready to throw away their garbage and the conflict starts. They keep collecting garbage for so many years and think that they have valuable things in their collection. But Saturn does not allow us to keep anything that has become waste.

So, Saturn removes the ego in Sade Sati because it is completely waste but people are not ready to throw it away. Then Saturn uses force and removes the cause of ego, so, people lose wealth, power, and position in their Sade Sati. After cleaning, that place starts shining, during that time many people get their lost things. Where dirt has suppressed life, it starts breathing again. That is why Sade Sati is not bad for everyone. The transit of Saturn clears everything, the waste has gone and now life can move forward.

Famous astrologer Dr. Nimai Banerjee has written that when Saturn transits from the seventh house to the tenth house, then such transit is very important in a person's life. Saturn fulfills the life's ambitions of the person and the person gets what he wants.

7.3 The Transit of Rahu & Ketu

Rahu and Ketu always move retrograde and complete one cycle in 18 years and stay in a sign for 1.5 years. The behavior of both these nodes is sudden, so when they change their sign unexpected events happen. The event triggered by them can affect the native for 1.5 years as they stay in that zodiac during that period.

The shadow planet Rahu is considered a curtain. At our home curtain prevents the sunlight from coming into the room and the room becomes slightly darker. When Rahu transit over the natal Sun then the sunlight becomes dim or when Rahu comes in front of the natal Sun then it works as a curtain and prevents sunlight from coming into that house. Due to the absence of sunlight, the problem related to the house starts which can last for 1.5 years.

After every 18 years, these two nodes return to the same position in the natal chart, then many significant changes happen in the life of the person. Rahu represents hunger and Ketu represents separation. These two nodes represent disturbed energies, where the nodes are placed the matter related to the house is always disturbed. The house in which, they are located in the birth chart, after 18 years when they return over there, the energy level would become high and unexpected events may happen related to the house concerned.

(**Note:** *With some additions the above article is taken from my book "Vedic Astrology: The Light of Wisdom".*)

Chapter 8

Wisdom from Ancient Scriptures

Vedic astrology is full of knowledge, various sages have contributed their knowledge in this field in different eras. The study of astrology is very broad and when a person goes deep into it, always he finds something precious in his hands. In this chapter I am describing the meaning of some important sutras from few ancient scriptures which I came across in my journey towards astrology.

8.1 The Two Kingdom - Zodiac Half

Saravali Volume 1, Chapter 3, Explanation of Sutra 9-10

The zodiac is divided into two parts or there are two kingdoms exist; the first part is ruled by the Sun and the second part is ruled by the Moon. From Leo to Capricorn consists the solar half and ruled by the Sun, from Cancer to Aquarius is the lunar half and ruled by the Moon. The Sun is considered as a King and assigned only one sign Leo, and the Moon is considered as a queen and assigned only one sign Cancer, rest of the planets from Mars to Saturn get one sign each in each kingdom.

In a natal chart, if the occupancy of the planets is more in the solar half then such a native has more masculine qualities, he is aggressive, courageous and prefer to take initiative. If the occupancy of the planets is in the lunar half then he has more feminine qualities. He is fortunate, receptive and soft-spoken person.

This sutra clearly indicates that there are two types of energy control the universe. Sun is ruler of the masculine energy and Moon is the ruler of the feminine energy and there is an equal division of power between the two. The existence is divided into two parts and the planets in the sky keeps on working to control all these things. Therefore, the scriptures say that being two is sorrow and being one is happiness and completeness is ecstasy.

8.2 Directions of Rashi

Saravali Volume 1, Chapter 3, Explanation of Sutra 22

Every direction denotes a rashi (sign) and the first four rashi indicate; East, South, West and North respectively and rest repeat in the same manner.

East – Aries, Leo and Sagittarius

South – Taurus, Virgo and Capricorn

West – Gemini, Libra and Aquarius

North – Cancer, Scorpio and Pisces

In horoscope, the 1st house indicates east, the 7th house indicates west, the 4th house indicates north and the 10th house indicates south. When Aries is rising in ascendant or when the Moon is transiting in Aries then when a journey started in east direction produces fruitful results and the same principle for others.

Note: It is necessary to identify the position of planets in a zodiac sign and the strongest planet in the horoscope, because their position and strength determine the direction of work.

8.3 Planetary Directions

Saravali states the (Vol-1, Chapter 4, Shloka 8), planetary rulership of the 8 quarters;

1. Sun – East

2. Moon – North – West

3. Mars – South

4. Mercury – North

5. Jupiter – North-East

6. Venus – South – East

7. Saturn – West

8. Rahu – South – West

8.4 Happy Midlife

Saravali Volume 1, Chapter 5, Explanation of Sutra 18

The sutra states that the person will live a happy life during midlife, if the lord of the Moon sign or the lord of the ascendant or Jupiter be in in Kendra houses (1, 4, 7, and 10).

My Experience: This sutra indicates that if any of the above three conditions are there in the natal chart of a person, then he will live a happy life during midlife. To know more about midlife crisis readers can refer my book "Midlife Crisis: An Astrological Approach".

8.5 Diva Bala and Ratri Bala (Day-Night Strength)

Saravali Volume 1, Chapter 5, Explanation of Sutra 41

The day-night strength is also known as Nathonnatha bala. It is part of Kala bala (time strength) under Shadabala. The sutra states that the day-night strength of a planet is capable of providing land, elephants, etc. Such a person courageously defeats his enemies and attains kingdom and wealth.

The strength of the planets is determined based on the time of birth of the native. Some planets are strong when born during the day and some at night. When the dasha of those planets comes which are strong in day-night strength, then significant changes take place in the life of the person.

Sun, Jupiter, and Venus are strong during the day, while Mars, Moon, and Saturn are strong during the night. Mercury is strong at sunrise and sunset.

In the above sutra, land and elephants represent prosperity and enemies indicate facing adverse circumstances in life. For example, if a person is born during the day then his Sun, Jupiter, and Venus are strong and when the dasha of these planets comes in his life then he gets strength and he achieves success. The same is the case with a person born at night. When the dasha of Mars, Moon and Saturn comes into his life then he is victorious and achieves prosperity in life, and the same is the case with Mercury.

8.6 The 9th House

Saravali Volume 2, Chapter 32, Explanation of Sutras 1, 2 & 3

This chapter deals with the ninth house which is the house of fortune, hence it should be strong. The house of fortune is the house counted from the ascendant or from the Moon, between the two the strongest should be taken into consideration. For example, if the ninth house from the Ascendant is an indicator of good fortune, then the inauspicious effects related to the ninth house from the Moon will also not be fully revealed.

The lord of the ninth house and the planet of the ninth house influence the fate of a person. Their strength or weakness indicates the strength or weakness of fate.

8.7 The 9th house is aspected by own Lord

Saravali Volume 2, Chapter 32, Explanation of Sutra 4 & 5

If the 9th house is aspected or occupied by its own lord then native gets flourish at his birth place. If other planets join the house or the house aspected by others then his fortune favors at some other place.

Sutra 5: If a planet full aspect the ninth house from the ascendant, the third house, or the fifth house then the person is extremely fortunate.

Every planet aspect the 9th house if it is situated in the 3rd house, but only Jupiter can aspect the 9th house from ascendant and the 5th house. It means if Jupiter is situated .

at ascendant or 5th house then it is highly fortunate for the person.

8.8 Jupiter in the 9th House

Saravali Volume 2, Chapter 32, Explanation of Sutra 6 & 7

If Jupiter is in the ninth house then the person will become a minister. If Jupiter in the 9th is aspected from the Sun then he is like a king; If due to the Moon he will be prosperous and enjoy pleasures; If from Mars, he will be endowed with gold; If by Mercury then he is affluent in speaking; If there is Venus then he will have quadrupeds, vehicles and money and if there is Saturn then he will have immovable property, asses and buffaloes.

8.9 Exalted Planet in the 9th House

Saravali Volume 2, Chapter 32, Explanation of Sutra 29

If a planet is exalted in the ninth house, then an excellent person is born with abundant wealth and gold. If the aspect of the benefic planet is on the exalted planet then the person will be the supreme ruler, destroyer of his enemies, having divine glory and great fame.

This sutra again emphasizes that the strength of the 9th house is important for good fortune.

8.10 Planetary Rays

Saravali Volume 2, Chapter 36, Explanation of Sutra 1, 2, 3, 4 & 5

Every planet other than Rahu and Ketu transmit their ray that is called planetary rays or Rashmi Bala. These rays determine the strength of the planet and thus the overall strength of the horoscope. Planets with higher number of rays give auspicious results whereas planets with a smaller number of rays unable to produce favorable results and cause harm.

There are two different schools of thoughts for calculation of planetary rays.

The First: In the exalted position the number of rays of the Sun is 10, that of the Moon is 9, that of Mars is 5, that of Mercury is 5, that of Jupiter is 7, that of Venus is 8 and that of Saturn is 5.

The Second: In the exaltation state all planets have 7 rays equally.

Most of the sages are of the opinion that there is equal distribution of 7 rays of each planet and all agree that it is zero at the point of debilitation.

Every planet attains its maximum strength when it is situated in an exalted position. When it moves towards its debilitation point the Rashmi Bala of the planet start reducing and at the debilitation point it does not produce any rays. The distance between exaltation and debilitation point is 180 degrees, which means that as the planet moves from exaltation to debilitation its Rashmi Bala start decreasing and when the planet moves from debilitation to exaltation its Rashmi Bala start increasing.

For example, Jupiter gets 7 rays when it is exalted in Cancer at 5 degrees and zero rays when it is debilitated in Capicorn at 5 degrees. Now we divide 180 degree by 7 and the result is 25? 42' 51.43". This means when Jupiter moves from Cancer to Capicorn after every longitude of 25? 42' 51.43" one ray is reduced and when Jupiter moves from Capicorn to Cancer after every longitude of 25? 42' 51.43" one ray increases.

There are 7 planets to be considered here and every planet have 7 rays; hence, for calculation of Rasmi Bala total point is 49. We have to find out the Rashmi Bala of every planet as per the above method and thus find out the overall strength of the horoscope.

8.11 Abhimukha and Paranmukha

Saravali Volume 2, Chapter 36, Explanation of Sutra 5, 28 & 29

The sutra further states that when a debilitated planet transits towards its exaltation point, the rays are

Abhimukha (facing upwards) and when an exalted planet transits towards its debilitated point, the rays are Paranmukha (facing downwards). Rays going upward mean favorable results and rays going downwards mean unfavorable results.

If there are Abhimukha rays on a planet, then it's said good effects will increase, whereas the Paranmukha rays will reduce the good effects. A larger number of rays multiply the result while a smaller number of rays reduce the effect. According to the rays, the total strength of the person and the insignificance or superiority of his effect is revealed.

8.12 Knowledge of Future

Phaladeepika states that (chapter 1, shloka 12), "Intelligence, knowledge of the future, traditional law, and Vedic knowledge are related to the 5th house."

The first house is related to the self or the present. The fifth house is related to the future, and the ninth house is related to the past. Man lives by knowledge and intellect. The fifth house is related to intellect and knowledge of the future, so it is related to speculation. The power of prediction and forethought comes from the fifth house. To examine the power of forethought, it is necessary to examine the 5th house from the lagna and the Moon, as well as the D9 chart.

Jupiter is the planet of wisdom, and it requires wisdom to anticipate the future. Therefore, Jupiter in the 5th house or its aspect on the 5th house is considered good for predicting events. Rahu is always interested in taking shortcuts; therefore, the position or aspect of Rahu in the 5th house indicates that the person will be interested in speculative activities.

8.13 Male & Female Planets

- Male Planets – Sun, Mars, Jupiter

- Female Planets – Moon, Venus

- Eunuch – Mercury, Saturn

The gender of planets plays an important role in deciding their nature. For example, a male cannot become aggressive in the presence of females. In the same way, male planets lose their aggression and behave like a female planet if surrounded by two female planets. For example, if Mars is present in lagna with the moon and in the second house, Venus is placed, then Mars will lose its aggression and show only gentle qualities.

Eunuch planets are harsh and show no mercy to anyone. Therefore, weak and afflicted eunuch planets indicate negative qualities of the person.

8.14 Sun, Saturn and Rahu

According to Sapta Rishi Nadi Astrology, these three planets are the agents of separation. Therefore, if two of these three influence a house, they separate the native from the traits of that house. For example, if two of these three are present in the 4th house, the person has to leave their home and often change their job. If they influence the 7th house, then the person has to face problems related to marriage. If it affects the 10th house, then the person's profession has been affected, and he often changes his job.

It is important to note that the significator of a house also affects the matters related to that house. Therefore, for the smooth functioning of the house, not only the dispositor, but also the significator (Karaka) must be in a good position. For example, the significator of the second house is Jupiter. So, if the significator, house, or dispositor is aspected by any two planets out of Sun, Saturn, and Rahu, then the person may face the problem of separation from family, or his savings may get affected.

8.15 Saturn Brings Paucity

Sapta Rishi Nadi further states that Saturn, in conjunction with Rahu, brings paucity. The sixth house is related to debt, as it signifies lack and deficiency. The second house is related to accumulated wealth. If the second house or its lord is under the influence of both

Saturn and Rahu, then the person faces debt-related problems in life. Such a person is unable to repay his debt for a long time. For example, if Mars, the lord of the second house, is placed in the seventh house and is aspected by both Saturn and Rahu, then the person faces not only a lack of money but also marriage-related problems.

If these two planets aspect the 4th house or its lord, then the person has to face lack of comforts at home.

8.16 Vehicles

In astrology, Venus, the planet responsible for vehicles, is considered a planet of luxury and comfort. Vehicles help people reach their destinations, providing comfort and ease to their feet and making travel easier. The fourth house in a horoscope is considered the house of comfort and Vahana Sthana (vehicle house). Therefore, a connection between the fourth house, the ascendant, and Venus indicates the acquisition of a vehicle.

The Role of Venus for the Acquisition of a Vehicle

- Venus is the main significator for Vehicle. Comfort, luxury, and happiness are associated with them.

- Therefore, a strong and well-placed Venus is necessary for the acquisition of a Vehicle.

The Role of the 4th House and Its Lord for the Acquisition of a Vehicle

The 4th house is related to happiness, comfort, and mental peace in life. It is related to the mother, roots, and ancestry. It signifies nurturing and emotional support, home, and family. It represents the private life of the person, and the placement of its lord indicates that the person likes to do activities of that house to get pleasure and happiness.

- A private vehicle provides space for private life.

- A vehicle provides comfort on a journey. People want a private vehicle so that they can travel easily with their family.

- Therefore, the 4th house and its lord play an important role in the acquisition of a Vehicle.

The Link

The relationship of Venus to the ascendant, the fourth house, or its lord, indicates that the individual will enjoy a vehicle in life. However, the type of vehicle or multiple vehicles depends on the strength of the deciding planets involved in the horoscope.

The Risk

When Venus or the fourth house is afflicted by malefic planets like Mars, Saturn, or Rahu, it indicates a high risk of accidents or loss. While benefic planets indicate safety and comfort in travel.

The Protection

Even if the horoscope is afflicted by malefic planets and there is a possibility of accidents, the person gets protection from any fatal accident if Jupiter has an aspect on the ascendant, fourth house, or Venus. Jupiter's aspect protects the person at the last moment, and the person narrowly escapes such accidents.

Example Chart

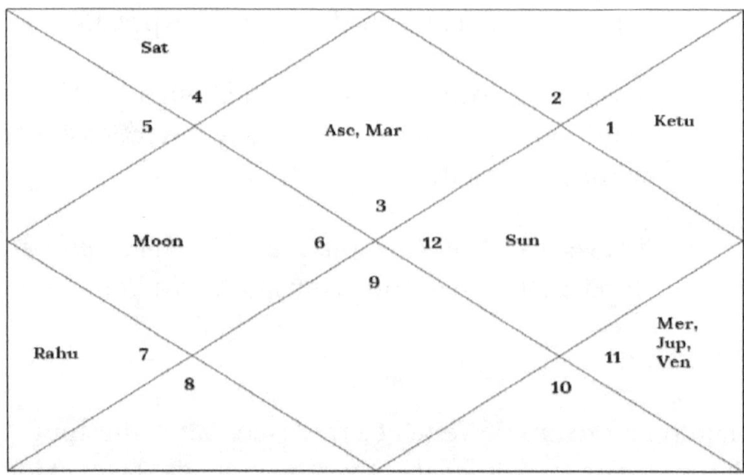

In the above horoscope, Mercury, the lord of the ascendant and fourth house, is in conjunction with Venus and Jupiter in the ninth house. This is a clear indication of vehicle ownership, and Jupiter, the planet of expansion, indicates multiple vehicles. Additionally, Jupiter's fifth aspect on the ascendant protects the native from any accidents.

Chapter 9

Astrology: Uses and Limitations

Knowledge of astrology cannot change the fate of a person but helps in taking steps in the unknown direction.

Man is always curious to know about the future. When a person opens his eyes, he is surprised to see the planets and stars in the sky. Everything is moving in a sequence and this constant movement affects every person. It is not easy for the human mind to understand this, but the mind wants to know this mystery. The science of astrology has evolved to understand these mysteries. Astrology is not like other science whose results can be tested in a laboratory. It is the study of invisible energy; therefore, it becomes subtle and demands not only knowledge but also the intuition of the individual.

One can study science by reading books and testing its results in the laboratory, but the same does not apply to astrology, because these results cannot be tested in laboratories. If a person simply reads astrological books and derives results verbatim, then he goes wrong and blames astrology for his wrong predictions. Therefore, intuition is important and one should not predict anything just by reading books if one's conscience does not support it.

In laboratory testing, the substance being tested is fixed and there is no possibility of entry of any other element while the process is going on, but this is not the case in astrology. Various subtle and invisible energies work together for an event to occur and its complexity is far beyond the understanding of the human mind.

The astrologer can only make a small effort to understand it, but everything is in the hands of God and it has to be accepted that there is a divine power spread all around which controls everything.

Therefore, astrology has its limitations and knowing every mystery behind every event is far beyond the human mind. However, one should leave no stone unturned to find it out. If the prediction is correct then one should consider it to be God's grace and should not feel proud and should not be disappointed if it is wrong. One must accept that all events are in the hands of the Almighty.

> **Astrology is not a means of entertainment that we get on television and newspapers, because entertainment has no solid basis and cannot last for generations.**

When dealing with astrology one should respect this great science and not ask questions for entertainment. Newspaper and television astrology have no meaning, it is only for entertainment purposes where curiosity is only related to some entertaining, a serious person should avoid all these activities. People are curious to know what kind of clothes he will wear, what kind of food he will eat etc. According to the author's opinion a serious astrologer should never answer all these worthless questions.

Also, an astrologer should not give answers to any person without asking any questions. If the person does not have a question then no answer has to be given. Knowledge of astrology is only for those people who are serious and looking for answers, because their life is stuck at the crossroads. Nature itself provides guidance to those who are serious about the answers and astrology is only a medium.

> *Knowledge of astrology is only for those people who are serious and looking for answers.*

This great science helps in understanding the mysteries of life. The transit of planets helps in understanding the principle of karma and the cycle of ups and downs in life. Everyone is happy with their upward journey and no one wants a downward journey in life, but the seed is sown only when you dig and go deep, the seed cannot be spread in the sky. Therefore, every cycle of life has its own meaning and with the help of astrology we can understand when it is time to step out and when it is time to keep dig deep and sow the seeds.

Just as 24 hours are divided into day and night, similarly every phase of life has its own meaning and without understanding astrology no one can understand the meaning of this cycle. As one enters this unfathomable ocean one realizes that everything here is connected and every individual is responsible for the seeds sown by him.

Therefore, such divine knowledge has enough potential to change a person forever, the constantly moving planets keep recording everything and return to the person with multiplications.

Astrology can reveal many secrets but it is not good to tell every secret to others. It is not necessary that the other person also understands the same meaning, people only listen to what is beneficial for them and when the predictions go wrong or things change in a negative way then they are immediately ready to blame. A person with a weak mind is not ready to assimilate the predictions. My experience is that if something happens in his favor he might stops his efforts and if something happens against him he gets afraid. Knowledge of the future frightens the weak minded and they break before time.

Astrology is not a science to satisfy one's greed. Therefore, one should never try to fool others by taking undue advantage of this science. Also, this knowledge should not be distributed to others for free. Because whatever knowledge people get for free, they will not respect it, neither will they respect astrology nor the astrologer. The one who knows, has a big responsibility to not let that knowledge go into the hands of wrong and greedy people.

The knowledge of astrology cannot change the fate of a person, but helps in taking steps in an unknown direction. Without proper direction, people keep wandering here and there in search of light, astrology can open many secrets and provide the true path of life.

A person is afraid of going in an unknown direction. Just as the signboards on the road show the way to a traveler, in the same way, with the help of astrology, a person is able to muster the courage to walk on unknown paths. But just as a person cannot be forced to travel if they don't want to, similarly, the mysteries can only be shared with those who are thirsty and seeking.

Great knowledge creates great responsibility, which is why our ancient sages have written down this knowledge in sutras and stories. Those who have the courage to move forward develop the ability to understand the meaning and for the rest it is only for entertainment.

> **Great knowledge creates great responsibility and requires courage to move forward.**

Sri Aurobindo has said, "The astrologer is born not made. It is impossible to manufacture a perfect astrologer by education as to manufacture a poet." (Vol. VII, Chapter – I)

Bibliography

Brihat Parashara Hora Sastra by Maharshi Parasara

Uttara Kalamrita by Kalidas

Mansagari, Translation by Shree Sitaram Jha, Shree Thakur Prasad Pustak Bhandar, Varanasi, India

Brihat Jatak, Translation by Prof. P.S. Sastri, Rajan Publications, New Delhi

Jatak Parijat, Translation by V. Subramanya Sastri, Rajan Publications, New Delhi

Hora Sara, by Prithuyasas (Translation by R. Santhanam)

Studies in Jaimini Astrology, Translation by B.V. Raman, MLBD, Delhi

Jaimini Sutram, Translation by Prof. P.S. Sastri, Rajan Publications, New Delhi

Jaimini Maharishi's Upadesa Sutra, Translation by Sanjay Rath, Sagar Publications, New Delhi

Saravali Vol 1 &2 (Translation by R. Santhanam)

Secrets of Predicting Dasha Results by Dr. Nimai Banerjee, Bhagyalipi Publications, Cuttack

Techniques of Predicting Future by Dr. Nimai Banerjee, Bhagyalipi Publications, Cuttack

Planetary Behavior & Human Life, Bhagyalipi Publications, Cuttack

About The Author

Ajay Srivastava is the founder of lotuswisdom.in and holds 'Bachelor of Science' from Deen Dayal Upadhyay Gorakhpur University, Gorakhpur (UP) and 'Masters Programme in International Business' from PSG Institute of Management, Coimbatore (Tamil Nadu).

He has extensive experience in the capital market as a Lead Analyst, Investment Banker, Consultant, and Advisor in identifying investment opportunities and formulating strategies. In his career, he has written various research notes and has done in-depth research from a commercial and financing point of view in multiple deals. With diverse industry experience and wide understanding, he started imparting his knowledge in the industry since 2013.

He has deep knowledge of graphology and since childhood he is very much interested in analyzing a person by handwriting and has analyzed the handwriting of hundreds of persons in his life.

He is very much passionate to learn about astrology and palmistry in deep and has completed 'JyotirVid' and 'JyotirVisharad' in Astrology from Bharatiya Vidya Bhavan, Mumbai. His various research articles have been published in the renowned Indian magazines "The Astrological eMagazine" and "Planets & Forecast".

Email ID: ajay.vastav@gmail.com

Web Site: http://www.lotuswisdom.in/

Books Written by the Author

1. Psychology and Investment

2. Vedic Astrology: The Light of Wisdom

3. Midlife Crisis: An Astrological Appraoch

4. Jupiter: The Planet of Fortune

5. The Joy of Creation and Success

6. The Light of Nakshatras

7. Sun: The Supreme Creator

8. Astrology & Predictions

9. Animal Symbols of Nakshatras

10. Astrology & Profession

11. Rahu & Ketu: The Invisible & Mysterious Planets

12. Planets & Human Life

Astrology Courses

1. Vedic Astrology for Beginners {Level – 1 (Basics)}

Module – 1: Basics of Astrology

Introduction; The Zodiac; Elements

Module – 2: Signs

Meaning of the Signs, Elements of the Signs, Qualities of the Signs, Odd and Even Signs, Sheershodaya & Prishtodaya Signs, Direction, Colors, Caste, Fruitful and Barren Signs, Masculine & Feminine Signs, Places, Other Major Qualities

Module – 3: Houses

Meaning of the 12 Houses, Types and Classifications of Houses

Module – 4: Planets

Planets and their Characteristics, Planetary Relationship, Exaltation, Debilitation & Mooltrikona, Natural Karakas, Karakas in Jaimini Astrology

Module – 5: Planets in Groups

Natural Benefic and Malefic Planets, Gender; Color; Caste; Guna and Places; Planet and Tastes; Nature of Planet; Elements; Metals; Age; Cloth and Height; Vegetable and Fruits; Physical Constituents and Tendency; Maturity Age of Planets; Planetary Aspects; Seasons; Hora

Module – 6: Planetary Strengths and Weaknesses

Strength of Planets based on its degrees, Direction; Direction Strength; Maran Karaka Sthana; Yog Karaka; Vargottam Planet; Shadabala

Module – 7: Retrograde and Combust Planet, Gandanta

2. <u>Vedic Astrology for Beginners {Level – 2 (Advanced)}</u>

Module 1: Vimshottari Dasha System

Nakshatra and Planetary Lordship, Change of Dasa and Results

Module 2: Basics of Nakshatra

Deity, Animal Symbol, Caste, Activity, Gana, Guna, Gender

Module 3: Important Yogas

Know the 30 most important astrological combinations

Module 4: Ashtakvarga

Interpretation of Ashtakvarga Table

Module 5: Transit of Planets and their impact

Understand the effect of transit of Jupiter, Saturn, Rahu-Ketu

Module 6: Planets and Profession

Identify the influence of the planet and the direction of profession

Module 7: Weak Planets and Remedies

Identify the signal of weak planets and useful remedies

Module 8: Key Steps to Chart Interpretation

Course Offerings:

· 30 hours of live sessions (Level 1 & Level 2)

· Learn various astrological concepts with practical examples

· Mode - Online Classes; Recordings available

3. <u>Nakshatra Course</u>

Knowledge of Nakshatra is very important in astrology, without it one cannot understand how energy works and what will be the result of the transit of planets. Do not limit yourself to the movement of planets, explore the world of Nakshatra and understand the hidden secrets.

What You'll Learn

• How the knowledge of Nakshatra helps to understand the characteristics and negative traits of the person

• Effect of transit of planets and time of activation

• Meaning of each symbol and its influence

• Influence of the associated animal on the personality of the person

• When to start a new venture and when not to go ahead

• Related Profession

• Understand each concept with logic

Course Offerings:

• 60 hours of live sessions

• Learn various astrological concepts with practical examples

• Mode - Online Classes, Recordings available

• Medium - English

Contact Us:

Mobile No.: +91 9867581379

Email ID: ajay.srivastava@lotuswisdom.in

Blog: https://lotuswisdomonline.blogspot.com/

4. A Course on Animal Symbols of Nakshatras

In the ancient scriptures, a total of 14 animals are related to the 27 nakshatras, and the behavior of every person is limited to these 14 animals. To understand the various merits and demerits of a person, it is necessary to understand the different characteristics of these animals.

How to Utilize Such Knowledge

• You will be surprised to know that these animals decide whom we form a relationship in our life.

• These animals determine our relationships with our friends, our spouse, our partners, our juniors and superiors.

• This knowledge helps to channelize your energy in pursuit of higher goals in life.

• The human mind is a very complex creation and it is difficult to say why a person behaves in a certain way and why his behavior changes. Knowledge of animal traits can provide proper guidance in this regard.

Course Offerings:

• 30 hours of live sessions

• Learn various astrological concepts with practical examples

• Mode – Online Classes; Recordings available

Sun:
The
Supreme
Creator
A Research Work on
Astrological Aspects of the Sun
Ajay Srivastava

The Light
of
Nakshatras
A Comprehensive Work to Explain the
Functioning of 27 Mystical Energies
Ajay Srivastava

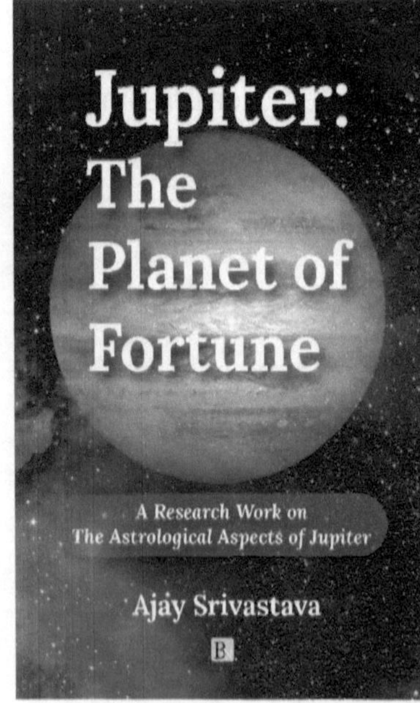

Jupiter:
The
Planet of
Fortune
A Research Work on
The Astrological Aspects of Jupiter
Ajay Srivastava

Vedic Astrology
The Light of Wisdom
Astrology for Beginners,
Learn the Language of Stars
Ajay Srivastava

Midlife
Crisis: An
Astrological
Approach
Understand The Timing Of Crisis,
Learn How To Turn A Crisis Into An Opportunity
Ajay Srivastava

PSYCHOLOGY
AND
INVESTMENT
The Art of Investing in Stocks with an
Explanation of Human Psychology
AJAY SRIVASTAVA

The Joy
of
Creation and Success
Ajay Srivastava

Astrology
&
Predictions
Ajay Srivastava

Animal Symbols
of the
Nakshatras
A Unique Book that Explains
the Relationship Between 14 Animals
Associated with the Nakshatras and Humans
Ajay Srivastava

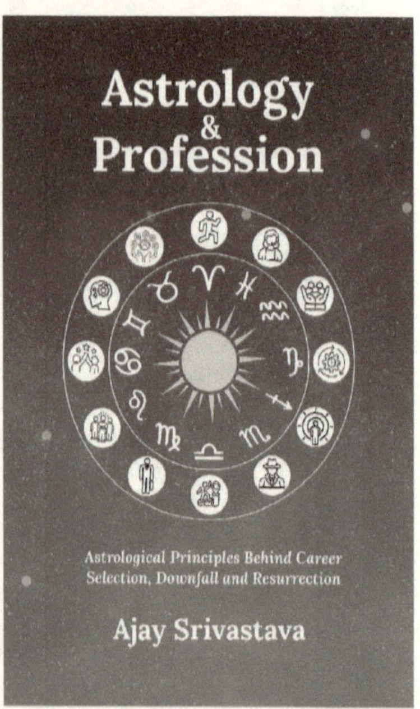

Astrology
&
Profession
Astrological Principles Behind Career
Selection, Downfall and Resurrection
Ajay Srivastava

Rahu & Ketu
The Invisible and Mysterious Planets
An Extensive Research Work to Demystify
the Mystery of Lunar Nodes
Ajay Srivastava

Planets
&
Human Life
A Research Work on The Impact of
The Nine Planets on Human Life
Ajay Srivastava

<u>Notes</u>

<u>Notes</u>